S0-ABQ-450

HILL WOMEN

HILL WOMEN

FINDING FAMILY AND A WAY FORWARD IN THE APPALACHIAN MOUNTAINS

CASSIE CHAMBERS

THORNDIKE PRESS
A part of Gale, a Cengage Company

Copyright © 2020 by Cassie Chambers.
Grateful acknowledgment is made to Pat Humphries for permission to reprint an excerpt from "Swimming to the Other Side" composed by Pat Humphries, © and ℗ 1992, published by Moving Forward Music. Reprinted by permission.
Thorndike Press, a part of Gale, a Cengage Company.

ALL RIGHTS RESERVED
Hill Women is a work of nonfiction. Some names and identifying details have been changed.
Thorndike Press® Large Print Biography and Memoir.
The text of this Large Print edition is unabridged.
Other aspects of the book may vary from the original edition.
Set in 16 pt. Plantin.

**LIBRARY OF CONGRESS CIP DATA ON FILE.
CATALOGUING IN PUBLICATION FOR THIS BOOK
IS AVAILABLE FROM THE LIBRARY OF CONGRESS**

ISBN-13: 978-1-4328-7917-4 (hardcover alk. paper)

Published in 2020 by arrangement with Ballantine Books, an imprint of Random House, a division of Penguin Random House, LLC

Printed in Mexico
Print Number: 01   Print Year: 2020

For my mother, Wilma

You don't go to Owsley County, Kentucky, without a reason. You can't take a wrong turn and accidentally end up there. It's miles to the nearest interstate, and there's no hotel in town. It doesn't cater to outsiders.

A half dozen times each year, I drive to Owsley County, where my mom grew up, and where, in many ways, I did too. The roads to this tiny Appalachian community wind tightly through the mountains, snaking around corners and plunging into valleys. Even after all my years of making the journey, I still feel a bit nauseous on some of the curves.

On this drive, I'm talking to one of my legal clients on the phone. "Yes, I'll meet you at the courthouse at eight A.M. Thursday," I yell, as though increasing my volume will make up for the patchy cell service. "Yes, eight A.M.!"

This client has called me repeatedly over the past few days, and this isn't the first time I've confirmed the time of her hearing. We are going to court to get a protective order to keep her safe from her physically abusive husband. I can tell she's nervous.

I start to say something to comfort her, but I'm interrupted by three short beeps letting me know that I have — once again — lost service. CALL FAILED flashes across the screen, and I can't help but feel as though this call isn't the only thing failing in my legal practice these days. I decided to work as a legal services lawyer in rural Kentucky to make a difference — to represent women who couldn't afford an attorney. Everything is harder than I'd anticipated. I sigh and switch on the radio.

Eventually the mountains give way to Booneville, the county seat and the only town for miles. From the top of the ridge I can see the town in its entirety, spanning just a few blocks, nestled in the holler below. I sigh again, this time with relief: It is always exactly how I remember it. There is comfort in that.

But once I'm driving in Booneville, surrounded by its smallness, there is a moment where the comfort resembles confinement. The town itself feels stagnant, silent, unchanging. Occasionally a pickup truck roars around the block and breaks the quiet. The stores are worn around the edges, with faintly painted signs and pitched awnings that flap against the gray sky. There is no trace of new business or development. The mega–chain stores so familiar to most Americans are nowhere to be found. Two dollar stores and two gas stations are the only franchises in town.

The local high school proclaims itself the "home of the Owsley County Owls." And that is how Owsley County is pronounced: "Owl-sley County." The order of the letters in the word doesn't really matter. People give little thought to such formalities.

The 1970s-style courthouse occupies the center of the town square. I occasionally go there for my work as a lawyer. When I do, I chuckle as I pass the sign inside that reads NO TOBACCO USE ALLOWED IN COURT-HOUSE. EXCEPT FOR THE OFFICE OF THE SHERIFF, COUNTY TREASURER, AND COUNTY CLERK. I used to think it was a joke, but a lawyer who works there assured me that it's not. They banned smoking in the courthouse just a few years ago, and I'm told some officials refused to go outside to have their cigarettes.

A plaque in front of the courthouse

proudly states Booneville's claim to fame: Daniel Boone once spent the night in the town square. Owsley County has another claim to fame: It is one of the poorest counties in America. According to the 2010 census, it has the lowest median household income — $19,351 — anywhere in the United States outside of Puerto Rico. More than 45 percent of the population lives in poverty. Only 38 percent participates in the labor force, and more than 20 percent has a disability. Even those numbers don't accurately describe how deep the poverty runs here.

It's not always visible, the poverty. Some parts of town are stacked with rows of neat brick ranches and freshly painted homes. One bright yellow house flies an American flag and has a beautiful birdbath in the front yard. Another has a border of flowering trees and well-manicured bushes. These parts of Booneville could be any small town in America.

But in some places the poverty is all that you can see: the places scattered with houses and trailers falling in on themselves, the structures so tilted and crooked it looks like a stiff wind might knock them over. The gaps in some of the wooden houses are visible from the road, and I'm told that at least a few of them still have dirt floors. At first glance, these places look abandoned. But a vehicle in the driveway is a marker that this sagging structure is someone's home.

It's hard for me to know which part of Owsley County I should show the rest of the world. Presenting the broken, falling-in places helps people understand the extent of the poverty. And I do want them to know how deep it goes. Maybe if they understand it, they can help fix it. But I also don't want them to think that this poverty is all that exists in Appalachia — to see Eastern Kentucky as hopeless, broken, dirty. That's not what I see when I look at this place that I love.

I round the square and continue driving. Along the way, some of the lawns are scattered with what appears to be junk: old car parts, refrigerators, children's toys. But I know that, for some people, the piles of seemingly useless stuff serve a purpose, and an entrepreneurial one at that. People here make a living however they can: selling old car parts, repairing refrigerators, organizing yard sales. They collect anything of possible value because they never know what will come in handy. If nothing else, they can sell the junk in a nearby town for fifty dollars a truckload. They are always thinking of ways to earn money, help a neighbor, provide for their family. There is drive, creativity, effort in unexpected places.

Some people look at this image of poverty with a sense of disgust: they see unkempt humans living in unkempt homes. Others view it with a sense of pity: those poor people, trapped in such awful circumstances. I try to look at it with a sense of respect: to remember how hard they are working to survive in the overlooked corner of the world they call home.

That last view of Owsley County feels the truest to me, even if the other views fit more easily into the categories outsiders want to create. For me, there is hope in the spirit of a people who find creative ways to exist in a community that has been systemically marginalized. In men and women who take care of each other even when the outside world does not take care of them. In people who broke their bodies in tobacco fields and coal mines to make a living in the only community they have ever known. We don't take time to see it: the hope in the poverty, the spark against the dreary backdrop, the grit in the mountain women.

I've come to know that grit well — that fire that fuels so many women in rural Kentucky. I see it every day in my clients:

women in the midst of a crisis, doing what it takes to keep themselves and their children safe. Once I recognized it, I saw its effects everywhere — the way it had shaped people, families, communities. The way it had shaped me.

Of course not everything in Owsley County is exceptional — exceptionally horrible, exceptionally virtuous, exceptionally whatever we want it to be. In many ways, it's ordinary, full of normal people living normal lives. These lives take a different shape and arc than they do in some other places, but the basic themes are the same. People care about love, community, family.

About a mile outside of town is a narrow gravel road that drops dramatically over the side of the hill, plunging steeply into the holler below. The holler is called Cow Creek; it shares its name with the stream that cuts through it. A few hundred yards farther and I'm at the bottom of this valley — a small, flat space enclosed by rolling hills. On the top of one of these hills is a farmhouse looking out onto the fields below.

The house resembles an elderly woman, leaning into itself, folding itself around an ever-weakening structure. It is gray now, its wooden boards faded and worn, but there are hints of the white and green it once wore. There is a strength in its brokenness. It has withstood weather, time, families. It is vacant now, resting, watching, waiting as each new day cascades into Cow Creek.

This holler feels like home, and this house feels like family. There are women's stories here, stories of resilience, love, and strength. This community knows them well, but their echo hasn't reached far enough into the outside world. Instead, these tales have ricocheted within the mountains, growing more faint with time. I want to tell these stories because they matter, because I'm afraid that they will be forgotten, because they have the power to make this community visible. As I stop my vehicle and walk toward the house, the memories wash over me like the sunlight on the mountain hills.

■ ■ ■ ■

PART I
HOME

■ ■ ■ ■

CHAPTER 1

The sun was directly over the Cow Creek holler, shining down onto the tobacco plants below. The summer heat was sticky, the type of heat that clings to your skin and makes your hair feel damp. I was standing in my grandparents' tobacco field, trying to shield my eyes from the incessant sun while holding an armload of tobacco sticks.

My five-year-old body was tired. I had been up since before five A.M., when my aunt Ruth lightly shook me awake. "Time to get up, Cassie," she'd said in a no-nonsense tone of voice. "There's work to be done."

That always seemed to be the case on the farm. So much work to be done.

Even at this young age, I knew I liked work — or at least that I was supposed to. Work was what kept the days full. What allowed me to bury my hands in the earth. What made me the same as my mother, my aunt Ruth, my Granny.

It didn't hurt that my aunt Ruth gave me a dollar for each day I helped out on the farm. I'm sure I was more of a hindrance than a help, my clumsy child hands fumbling through tasks. But she was teaching me an important lesson, one that generations of mountain women have learned before me: There is value in work. Hard work pays off.

At the end of the week Aunt Ruth would take me to town. We would stop at yard sales along the main road, or perhaps wander into the Family Dollar store. I would spend my hard-earned money on a used doll or a bag of candy, or some other trinket. And, pushing my wadded-up bills across the counter, I would feel proud.

I released one tobacco stick onto the ground below and continued walking through the rows of plants, scattering the tobacco sticks as I went.

Up ahead I saw my aunt Ruth, bent over in the field. Aunt Ruth was the best tobacco worker in Owsley County. Even the men said so. She could cut more stalks per hour than the strongest man. She rarely stopped to rest.

Watching her move through the fields ahead of me, I was struck by her solidness, the strength of her body. Even then I could see that she mirrored the mountains rising up in the distance. I was also struck by her grace. The way she knew the land. The deftness and ease she carried to each task.

"How ya doin' back there, Cassie?" she shouted from up ahead.

I was fine. I was content. I was at peace in this holler in the hills.

The sun sank toward the edge of the mountains, and our time in the fields drew to a close for the day. We made our way from the tobacco fields to the green-and-white farmhouse nestled on a nearby hill. We sat on the front porch to rest before beginning the evening chores. The porch's tin roof was rusted, and the wooden floorboards sagged in places. The attached house looked tired, even then, edges and joints giving way. But pots of bright wildflowers sat along the front rail, their long stems woven into a net of green and color. They made the old house something alive, something beautiful. Aunt Ruth loves to plant wildflowers.

Aunt Ruth has not had an easy life. Born in 1958, she was the fourth of seven children and the firstborn girl. My mother would come along — years later. Ruth, like the rest of her siblings, began working in the tobacco fields at an early age. She liked working on the farm — liked working with the earth — and she made it a point to outwork her brothers.

She had once dreamed of something beyond the tobacco fields. She had wanted to graduate from high school — to be the first in her family to get an education. But when she was about sixteen she got rheumatic fever and had to stay home from school for a year. She had attended school sporadically before that, and, with no plan to keep current on her lessons, she felt like it would be impossible to ever catch up. She decided that she had been silly to dream of anything more.

So Ruth set out to achieve in the only way that she could: becoming the best worker in Owsley County. It was one of the few paths she had to gain recognition, to feel pride. Day after day, year after year, she worked on the farm. Cutting her hair short to keep it from matting against her neck. Wearing heavy jeans even in the summer heat. Breaking her body to contribute to her family.

Over the years her siblings moved off of the farm, got married, started families of their own in other parts of Owsley County. Ruth remained behind. She knew that her aging parents couldn't manage the farm without her. She knew that she was the best worker in the family. She knew it was her job to keep the farm afloat.

That's not an easy thing to do as a share-cropper. Our family didn't own the land we worked — we never did. We rented the house, the barns, the fields, from the Reed family. At the end of each planting season, we gave half of the tobacco earnings to the Reeds for rent. If it was a good year, my family may have gotten to keep a little less than ten thousand dollars. The constant repairs to the house, need for new farm equipment, and other daily expenses de-pleted that money quickly. Aunt Ruth took on odd jobs — mowing lawns for neighbors and washing cars in town — to help make ends meet.

After we sat on the porch for a bit, Aunt Ruth stood up and told me it was time for chores. I scampered behind her to the barns, where we tended to the animals. More accurately, Aunt Ruth tended to the animals while I tried to track down the new-est litter of barn kittens. One of the old barn cats had given birth earlier that week, and she kept moving her kittens from place to place, probably to keep them safe from my unwanted cooing and petting.

I loved the smell of the barn. Even now I

can smell it if I close my eyes, the scent of cool and earth and animal.

The sun had barely set when it was time to get ready for bed. There was no indoor plumbing, so I used well water to brush my teeth and wash my dirt-covered body the best I could. Every few days Aunt Ruth filled up a tin tub with hot water so I could take a bath.

Aunt Ruth walked with me to the outhouse and shone a flashlight inside the lopsided hut before I went in. The other day, Granny had said that the neighbors found a black snake in their outhouse. The thought of a snake — even a harmless black snake — lurking in the dark terrified me. Aunt Ruth put a big bucket in the house for us to use as a nighttime toilet so no one had to trek to the outhouse in the pitch dark.

That night I crawled into bed next to Aunt Ruth. She told me stories about the haunted holler, and our kinfolk, and the mountain people. Storytelling is an art in the mountains, a way of transmitting history, culture, and shared experience from generation to generation. She told me stories about my mother as a child, the ghosts in the woods, and quick-witted hill people. I listened raptly to her yarns until my eyes grew heavy and my lashes knitted together.

I would spend several more nights here, in Owsley County, that week. I would probably spend several nights the next week. Both my mother and father were students, young parents, struggling to build a better life for me. They couldn't afford childcare, and there was nowhere I would rather be than this patch of earth in the mountains. I often came for a week at a time; my mother says that, as a young child, there were periods when I was here more than anywhere else. I can't remember a time when I wasn't frequently running through the Cow Creek holler.

And I rarely ran alone. There was a slew of kids to get into trouble with. My cousins — Melissa, Ben, and Dustin — are all around the same age as me, and our family relationship mandated that we become friends. Family was important — all of our parents believed so, and they made sure we spent time together, "gettin' to know your kinfolk," as Granny liked to say.

Melissa, just a few months older than me, was my best friend. We would catch crawdads in the creek and play with dolls in the living room. The boys, Ben and Dustin, would drive us crazy with their wild antics and roughhousing ways. Even as young children they were taught to embody a type of tough masculinity that drew suspicious glances from us girls. We would sneak off into the fields to pick wildflowers and hide when we heard them coming.

Aunt Ruth was often charged with supervising us. She had a matter-of-fact approach to life and childcare. "Well, of course that dog bit you," she once told a crying Ben. "I told you not to pull his ears. That'll teach you not to bother that dog no more." She raised her eyebrows at him and went back to work. She was a busy woman, doing what it took to keep the remaining family afloat. She didn't have time to fuss over us, and she believed that children learned from the natural consequences of their actions. But we never doubted that she loved us something fierce.

I had spent the morning playing in the creek that cuts across the cow pasture, moving the flat rocks around, trying to build a dam. It was hot, and I was on my way to the house for a glass of water. As I rounded the corner I saw Granny, limbs akimbo, standing awkwardly in a tree. Grannies were not supposed to climb trees. My jaw dropped open a bit.

"Cassie, git me a jar," she hollered, her voice raised and filled with excitement.

"Your Granny's about to git you a tree frog!"

I had been wanting a pet frog. I listened to them singing in the evenings and ran from corner to corner of the yard trying to find them. I never imagined, though, that I would come to acquire one through my Granny's acrobatic prowess.

Granny's hands closed swiftly and softly around something on a tree branch, and she made the short drop to the ground below, tree frog in hand. Her eyes twinkled from behind her thick glasses as she said, "Ah, boy! We've got 'im!"

Granny found joy in the simple things. In a Ralph Stanley cassette tape playing while she swept the house. In a neighbor stopping by for a short visit. In helping a granddaughter get a new pet. She celebrated each moment that stood out against the backdrop of challenge and struggle.

Housework filled Granny's days. Without indoor plumbing, she had to travel back and forth to the well to get water for tasks like washing dishes and doing laundry. The wood-fired stove that she cooked on was cantankerous, and it was hard to keep it from getting too hot and burning the food. The house was heated by a single coal stove. In the winter, Granny sometimes woke up before four o'clock to stoke the fire.

By the early 1990s, hard work was the usual for Granny. From the time she was a child growing up on a farm, she was expected to help out in the fields and the house. There was little time for fun or rest. Granny never played a sport or went to a friend's house or the movies. She never watched television or had a doll or ate ice cream. Instead, she picked beans, made corn bread, and milked cows. She attended school on and off until she dropped out in the third grade.

Even with her brothers and sisters pitching in, resources were scarce. There were times when she and her six siblings went hungry. The house they lived in — a few miles from Cow Creek — was old, and the single fireplace couldn't keep it adequately heated in the winter. Some mornings she would wake up to find her blanket covered in frost.

Yet somehow she learned to find joy in it all. I know this because I saw it: the way joy always flowed so easily and freely through her. She hummed as she cooked. She danced as she cleaned. She laughed clearly and frequently.

Her joy hid the poverty. I didn't know that the walls of the farmhouse on Cow Creek were made out of cheap particleboard or that having walls made out of particleboard was anything to be ashamed of. I didn't understand that the tin roof was in desperate need of repair. I didn't realize that some kids would turn up their noses at the bologna sandwiches we had for lunch some days. Years later, I would learn that bologna sandwiches had been a rare and expensive treat when Ruth and my mother were growing up, and I would feel bad for taking them for granted.

But it also didn't *feel* as though we were poor. Granny was generous. She offered anyone passing through Cow Creek a meal or a piece of cake. Once, a man came electioneering, asking Granny for her vote. "Son, you know I can't vote for you," she said mirthfully, " 'cause you's a Republican, and I don't mess with that foolishness. But if you come on up to the house I got a piece of pie that you're welcome to." Granny had spent all day working on that pie, a special treat for her family, but this man looked hungry, and Granny wouldn't abide hungry people walking around Cow Creek.

The evening after the frog capture we were watching the old television in the living room. It was finally working again, thanks to Granny's efforts. She had taken it apart and fixed it herself that afternoon. I had watched as she laid out the pieces carefully, her blue eyes squinting as she thought. I doubt a trained television repairman could've done a better job. In my mind, there was nothing Granny couldn't fix.

A few days later, I heard a car rumbling off in the distance, the sound of crunching gravel bouncing off the mountains. I ran down the hill from the house to the road, hoping to make out the color of the car as it rounded the bend. Before I knew it I could feel it: it was my mother. I ran to her as soon as the car stopped.

My mother, Wilma, is beautiful. At that time, she had permed blond hair; strong, tanned legs; and Granny's — her mother's — sparkling eyes. Her speech was fast, accented, carrying the tone and rhythm of the mountains.

In many ways, Wilma took after Granny. She had her same easy smile and her same fiery temper. It would flare quickly, burn brightly, then extinguish as fast as it had arrived. As a child, she fought ferociously with each of her four brothers. She once threw an empty gallon orange-juice container twenty yards while running, to bean her brother Dale in the back of the head. She whacked another brother with a fireplace poker when he messed with her pet cat. She wasn't afraid of a fight.

She was also incredibly kind. When our pet dog went blind, she made sure to keep everything in the house the same so that the dog could find her way around. She cried when the monster died in the movie *Godzilla* because it pained her to see any living creature suffer. She always told me, "You get more flies with honey than vinegar." I would come to see that Wilma embodied the delicate balance of so many mountain women: kind, gentle, firm, unyielding, capable of erupting into fire under the right circumstances.

Wilma, like Granny before her, was well acquainted with hard work as a child. She would get up at four or five o'clock to help cook breakfast before the others woke up. The house was drafty, and it could be an hour before it was warm enough not to see your breath in the winter air. Once the morning meal was done, Wilma would clean the kitchen and join the others — including Ruth — in the fields by seven A.M. Other than a short lunch break, she worked straight through until four in the afternoon. Then she and her siblings would complete their chores, play tag or softball in the yard, and go to bed. The next morning she would do it all again.

I was excited, as I always was, to see my mother that day in the mountains. We loaded my few things into the old car and began the drive home. We lived in Berea, less than fifty miles from Owsley County, but the hills and curves made it seem much farther. Along the way I told my mother about my adventures on the farm: the places my dog, Bubbles, and I explored, the way I helped Granny make the corn bread, the tree frog that Granny and I caught and later released. She listened carefully, asked questions, and told me she was glad I had fun.

A little over an hour later, we arrived. Berea is set in the foothills of the mountains, at the western edge of Appalachia — the last county that the Appalachian Regional Commission considers part of Appalachia proper. This small town has always been a place ahead of its time, in large part because of Berea College. Founded in 1855 by the abolitionist John Fee, Berea opened its doors to students of all races and both genders from the outset. In 1866, the year after the Civil War, ninety-six of its students were black and ninety-one were white. Today, one in three students is a person of color, and the school enrolls students from more than sixty countries. The progressive values embodied by Berea College have seeped into the surrounding community. Full of artisans, international craft markets, and eclectic musicians, Berea feels different — more diverse and colorful — than many people expect Appalachia to be.

Undergirding this diversity is a distinctive mountain feel. Most of Berea's students, more than 70 percent today, come from Kentucky or Appalachia. The average student's family makes less than $30,000 per year, and over half are first-generation college students. That reflects the school's mission: to provide a free college education to low-income Appalachian students. Instead of paying tuition, students participate in a work-study program, where they are employed as teaching assistants, restaurant workers, and folk artisans. My mother, in her early days at Berea, worked as a weaver. Another friend of hers learned to make baskets by hand. Even now, a quilt made in Berea is a prized possession of many a Kentuckian.

Young people flock to Berea because of the college's combination of quality and affordability. In an age of increasing college debt, a free education is a hard thing to come by. With them, these students bring their music, their food, and their art. The college, and, subsequently, the town, celebrates this unique culture, a blend of the mountains and countries far away. The campus occupies the center of town, the heartbeat that energizes the surrounding community.

Once we were home that evening, I played in the living room while my mother studied for her college classes. The worn carpet in our apartment became mountains and valleys where my plastic animals frolicked. I was good at entertaining myself. As an only child, I learned early how to keep myself occupied. I once spent an entire afternoon watching a line of ants build a mound.

While I played on the floor, my mother sat above me on the couch, surrounded by yellow notepads and open library books. I asked her a question, and it took her a minute to pull her thoughts away from the book she was bent over. A few hours later my father returned from his classes, and we built a zoo underneath the coffee table.

My mother was almost finished with her college degree. After taking evening classes at a nearby school for a couple of years, she had recently gone back to Berea as a full-time student. Despite being the second youngest of her seven siblings, she would soon become the first in her family to graduate from college, just as, a few years before, she was the first in her family to finish high school. Lying on our living room floor, I knew that my mother would study late that night, as she did many nights. She would tuck me in to bed, read me a book, and then return to the living room. There she would write papers and tackle homework assignments. In the middle of the night I would sometimes sneak out of bed and tiptoe down the short hallway. I would watch my mother, brow furrowed, seeking a way forward in the pages.

They are strong mountain women, Aunt Ruth, Granny, my mother. When I was a child, it seemed as though they could bend the world to their will. I never once heard them say "I can't do that." They also never directed those words at me. Once, when I was seven or so, I told Granny "I want a cucumber," expecting her to hand me one from the basket of vegetables on her lap. "Well, over there's a whole field of them," she replied. "Honey, go get you as many cucumbers as you want." Off to the field I went.

They modeled independence, hard work, persistence. They took care of me, of one another, and of their communities. They embodied the strength and security of the mountains that surrounded them. It's no wonder I grew up thinking I could take on the world. But it is still a wonder to me that I was able to in the ways that were to come.

I don't have enough ways to honor them, these women of the Appalachian hills. Women who built a support system for me and for others. The best way I know is to tell their stories.

CHAPTER 2

I was born in the fall of 1986. I had my father's bright red hair and my mother's quick-to-flare Eastern Kentucky temper. I screamed most of the time I was in the hospital.

My parents, Wilma and Orlando, were young, still students. They had gotten married a little less than a year before, and they hadn't counted on having a baby so soon. When my mother told my father they were pregnant, he joked, "Well, I suppose we will just have to put her out to pasture if we want to feed her." His joking hid his very real, very palpable concern: babies cost money, something they didn't have.

Wilma and Orlando had met when Wilma was a freshman at Berea College. Owsley County High School had left Wilma unprepared for Berea's rigorous curriculum, so the college made her take a few remedial courses her first semester. One of these, to

Wilma's numerically challenged horror, was math.

It was there that she met my father.

Orlando was born in Ohio, in a small town about an hour from Cincinnati. His family has deep ties to Eastern Kentucky: his grandfather was born in Lee County, which shares a border with Owsley. His family had lived in Eastern Kentucky since the mid-1800s, but Orlando's grandfather left the mountains in the early 1900s, part of a wave of people who left the hills in search of better opportunities in more industrial cities.

In many ways, this plan paid off for Orlando's family. Orlando's father worked in a factory, earning a blue-collar living with a good manufacturing job. His mother was a homemaker. Like Wilma, Orlando grew up in farm country, but in an area with far less poverty. There was a movie theater and a Kmart less than ten miles away. He and his siblings got to go to restaurants occasionally. Everyone always had plenty of clothes and food.

Wilma's family, on the other hand, grew most of their food, and it wasn't until she was in high school that Granny treated them to a store-bought frozen pizza. Almost all of Wilma's clothes were secondhand, given by churches and neighbors. When she was young, she asked Granny why Santa Claus hated her, since she and her siblings never got toys for Christmas.

Orlando was a couple of years ahead of Wilma in college. He had bright red hair that curled around his ears and always had a crinkle across the front from putting on a baseball cap right after showering. He was a math major and the teaching assistant assigned to Wilma's section of remedial math.

Wilma was in a bad mood that first day of class. The first week of orientation had been exhausting. She missed home. Everything was unfamiliar. Berea, and its few thousand students, seemed overwhelmingly large. She was afraid to leave her dorm room because she wasn't sure she could find her way back. Even amongst her fellow Appalachian students her heavy Owsley County accent stood out. She entered the classroom right as the bell rang and plopped unhappily into her seat.

Once the class was seated, Orlando called the roll. One by one, the students answered "Here." When he reached Wilma's name, she responded, with too many vowels, "He-arrre."

Orlando paused. He looked at Wilma and asked, "Where are you from?" Her accent was distinctive, and he was curious to know more about the attractive blonde in the second row.

Wilma, normally timid and polite around strangers, had had enough. Her mountain-woman temper flared. "Why did you ask me that?" she said defiantly, her accent growing stronger.

Orlando, a consummate conflict avoider, quickly lowered his eyes to his roll sheet. "Never mind," he said, his voice just a touch higher than it had been a minute earlier. He tried to move on to the next name on the roll list.

"No," Wilma said. "I want to know why you asked me where I'm from. You didn't ask anyone else where they were from. You think I talk funny, don't you?"

"Oh . . . no . . . goodness, no," Orlando stammered. By now his cheeks matched his red hair. He averted his eyes and quickly called the next name on the list. "Sara? Do we have a Sara in the class today?" Wilma, seething in her seat, decided to let him move on unimpeded. He was, after all, she thought, somewhat handsome.

From then on, Wilma and Orlando saw each other three times a week in Math 015. Wilma decided Orlando was cute and kind. Orlando decided Wilma was beautiful and a bit terrifying. Their initial confrontation soon transformed into a mutual crush.

Wilma threw herself into her math studies with unprecedented vigor. Each night, she would wrestle her way through her homework, double-checking every answer. The next day, in class, she would call over Orlando to "help" her with the completed problems. As he explained things, she replied, "Oh, yes, I get it now." She liked having an excuse to interact with him, and she liked the way he smelled. Eventually they began to date.

On their one-year anniversary, Orlando emptied his savings account. He bummed a ride to a local shopping mall to buy a ring and invited Wilma to dinner at the restaurant where she worked. Orlando had told their friends he was planning to propose that night, and the group had been stealthily creeping up and down the street, hoping to catch a glimpse of the proposal through the window. Orlando asked Wilma to marry him, and a smile — half glee, half surprise — spread across her face. After it was clear she had said yes, their friends celebrated in the street.

Wilma and Orlando decided to schedule the wedding for just a couple of months after the proposal. She was nineteen and he was twenty-one. Neither saw any reason to wait. They both came from places where family was valued more than anything. They were both eager to start a family themselves. A few months after the wedding, Wilma, worried and exhilarated, told Orlando that they were expecting a child.

Now, when I ask my parents how they felt in that moment, they tell me they were terrified. But they say it with a whimsical smile that makes it seem like they weren't really that afraid — like a pair of teenagers fondly recounting the moment the roller coaster balanced at the top of the hill before plunging, at full speed, toward the bottom. And I suppose that's what they were in that moment: young people at a precipice, looking over an edge. They didn't know what this ride had in store for them, but — as young people so often do — they assumed that everything would be fine in the end.

Figuring out how to pay for my birth was the first of many struggles for the young couple. They had little money, and they had trouble finding an obstetrician in the area who would accept their government-issued medical card. "Sorry, we only take private insurance," each of my mother's top choices of doctors told her.

In the 1950s and 1960s, Granny had also

40

struggled to get medical care while pregnant. There were no doctors near Cow Creek at that time, and Papaw, her husband, didn't have a vehicle — or the knowledge to operate a vehicle — to fetch a doctor. Nor did they have a telephone to call for help. Instead Papaw would walk, sometimes miles, sometimes in the middle of the night, once in snow up to his waist, to the nearest midwife. The midwife would come to Cow Creek, and Granny would give birth at home. Midwives like these were called "granny midwives," and they received little or no formal medical training. They learned from the previous generation how to care for the women in their community.

Granny came down with measles during her second pregnancy. No one had told her that measles could harm her unborn baby, so she hadn't thought a lot about it when she first fell ill. Even if someone had told her of the risks, it wouldn't have mattered — there wasn't a lot Granny could've done to avoid this disease, which ran unchecked through mountain communities. The child of that pregnancy, a son named Herbert, died suddenly a few months after his birth. Granny felt guilty for years afterward, wondering if her measles had led to his death. She wondered if there was something she could have done to save him.

There wasn't. Maternal and infant mortality rates were high in those days. There was little access to formalized medicine. Very few women received prenatal care; even the *idea* that pregnant women needed a unique type of care hadn't penetrated many mountain communities. Many granny midwives relied on folklore and invasive practices. The most popular means of pain management was to place an ax under the bed to "cut the pain of labor."

Despite these dangerous and disparate conditions, women in the mountains cared for one another. In communities where women were perceived as having less power, birth was a time for them to publicly exercise what power they had. One woman described childbirth as the "one occasion when the women took over. No men were allowed. . . . This happy time was known as a 'granny frolic.' . . . Every married woman friend and relative was welcome." It was a time for women to come together to celebrate one another and new life.

They shouldn't have had to do it, these women. To try to care for one another with such limited resources. To be responsible for filling a role that modern medicine filled in other parts of the country. To mitigate risk in a system of such disparity. But they did do these things, and they did them to the best of their ability. Some people see the statistics on the health outcomes in Appalachia during this time and they are shocked by the disparity with more affluent parts of the United States. I am shocked that, in these communities of such limited resources, the disparities were not even worse than they were.

A woman named Eula Hall lived in Eastern Kentucky, a few counties away from Owsley, birthing and raising children at around the same time as Granny. One of Eula's children was born premature and deaf; another child died in infancy. She saw families torn apart by lack of healthcare: children left motherless after a woman died in childbirth, parents suffering the loss of a child from routine childhood illnesses such as strep throat or tetanus.

Eula set out to take charge of the situation. As she told me years later, "We was livin' in hell, so I decided it was time for me to raise hell." In 1973 she took a $1,400 donation and turned it into a health clinic — sometimes operating out of her own home — that provided care to low-income Eastern Kentuckians.

When the clinic burned down in 1982,

Eula went door-to-door raising money to reopen it. In the meantime, she had the phone company attach a telephone to a tree by the river so that she could operate the clinic outdoors. The phone company initially told her that they could not, under any circumstances, put a telephone on a tree. But Eula let them know in no uncertain terms that that answer was unacceptable. "You put telephones outside for the coal mines," she told them. "You will put a phone outside for me." The clinic never missed a day of operating.

I met Eula in 2018, when my work with low-income women led us to cross paths. At ninety years old, she was still working every day. The clinic she started was still seeing patients, and Eula operated a food pantry to help struggling families make ends meet. She told me about a man who had come in that morning. He hadn't eaten in three days, and Eula sent him home with a bag of food. Her original clinic had grown into a network of clinics, providing healthcare to over 200,000 community members — including many new and expectant mothers — a year.

My mother didn't go to Eula's clinic when she found out she was pregnant. She didn't know about it, and even if she had, she couldn't have made it there. That clinic was several counties away from where she lived, and Wilma didn't have a driver's license.

But my twenty-year-old mother had inherited the mountain-woman instinct to fight for her family, and her experience at Berea College had added a modern flavor to this intuition. She knew that she needed quality maternal healthcare; she had learned in her child-development classes just how crucial that care was. She showed up at the doctor's office ready to find a creative solution.

"I know you don't take Medicaid," Wilma told her top-choice doctor, a look of resolve in her eye, "and I don't have the money to pay you up front. But I do promise that I'll pay for your services myself. I can't afford it all right now, but I'll pay it in installments."

The doctor, perhaps struck by the determination in this young soon-to-be mother's eyes, agreed to her proposal. Wilma set up a payment plan, and she and Orlando scrimped and saved. Orlando took a job at a fast-food restaurant and existed on a diet of ramen noodles. They sold some things and did without others. They paid the final balance to the obstetrician shortly before I was born. "We paid you off just in time to take you home," my mother teases me.

My parents brought me home from the

hospital to a rented trailer located near the edge of Berea. It was too cold in the winter and too hot in the summer. It had a window air-conditioner unit, but my parents couldn't afford to run it.

In the fall of 1986, my father had just graduated from Berea and started graduate school in agricultural economics at the University of Kentucky. He had been accepted into many graduate programs, including one in the Ivy League, but I'm not sure anywhere outside of Kentucky was ever on the table. Wilma couldn't stand the thought of moving farther away from her family, and the couple needed help with their new baby. They stayed in Berea, within easy driving distance of Owsley County.

As a graduate student, Orlando received a stipend of $583 per month. My mother took a couple of years off from school to stay home with me, and during that time our entire family lived off of that small sum. Paying the bills each month was difficult — babies are not cheap and, since Orlando had graduated and Wilma was no longer a student, the couple didn't qualify for student housing.

I didn't realize then how tight money was. My mother had to save up to be able to buy me a pack of old maid cards from Walmart.

46

Sundays, after church, was the only time we would go out to eat. My parents would buy a Happy Meal at the local McDonald's. We would all share the small amount of food, my parents splitting the cheeseburger while I ate a few of the french fries and played happily with my new toy.

My mother always says we couldn't have survived in those days without our Owsley County family. Papaw would offer to buy her gas and give us buckets of vegetables from the garden if we would come down for the day. So three or four days a week my mother loaded me into my car seat to go to Owsley County. As I got older and my mother went back to college, I spent time there by myself.

I know it was hard for my mother to leave me, even for just a few days at a time. Berea was my home base, and even though my parents were busy students, with homework and midterms, I always felt like I mattered to them. They always had time for a round of "go fish" or choreographing a dance routine. But from the time I was old enough to talk, I would ask to go to Owsley County — to be with the farm and the mountains — and my mother knew that I would learn more there than I would in daycare. I learned science from watching the tomatoes grow, engineering from helping repair a fence, art from watching Aunt Ruth quilt in the evenings.

Owsley County was different for me than it was for my mother and her many siblings. Although I had cousins to get into trouble with, they were just that: cousins. Most evenings they would go back to their own houses after we spent the day playing. I was never lonely, but I was sometimes alone.

My mother was one of seven kids. J.L., the oldest son, was a rambunctious first addition to the family clan. Herbert, the second child, died when he was an infant. Vernon, the third, was proud and quick to anger. Ruth, the fourth-born, was a tomboy who preferred fieldwork to housework. Dale, the fifth child, was jolly and quick-witted. Wilma, my mother, was the sixth to come along. Charlie, the last, was and will always be the baby of the family.

The children fought like banshees amongst themselves, but they fiercely defended one another against any outsider. Ruth once beat up a boy a head taller than her who had picked on Charlie at school. Dale threatened Wilma's boyfriends with various types of shooting if they mistreated her. In the evenings, they played kickball together in the front yard. They were a tight-knit group. Granny sometimes showed me a box with a few of their toys in the attic, and Aunt Ruth constantly told me stories about their escapades. "That right there is where yer mommy pushed Dale into the creek," she would say as we walked through the holler in the evenings. "It's a wonder she didn't kill 'im!"

When I wasn't at Cow Creek, I spent a lot of my time on the campus of Berea College, especially once my mother went back to school full time when I was four years old. The college had a daycare for children of students and faculty that I sometimes attended. One of her friends picked me up at the end of the day and walked me over to the academic buildings to wait for her. I made friends with the college students I met en route. "Hello! I'm Cassie," I would say as I waved vigorously. "Have a good class!" My mother says that when we ate at the campus dining hall, more people knew me than her. I would take her hand and drag her up to different tables, saying, "Come meet my new friend!" I was as comfortable at the college as I was in the tobacco fields.

But my mother was not.

In some ways, it's amazing that Wilma decided to finish college. She had been looking for an excuse to drop out of Berea from the time she'd enrolled. She hadn't wanted to attend and ended up there thanks only to pressure from Granny and Aunt Ruth. She assumed that she would go to school for a semester, maybe two. With a husband and a child, she certainly had reason to put her education on an indefinite hold. Plus, things continued to be tight financially. So tight that once, my father had to break my piggy bank to afford a water pump for the car. It would've been easy for Wilma to have given up and gotten a full-time job.

But being at Berea changed Wilma. She was in an environment where everyone around her expected to get college degrees. Her peers viewed a degree not as an impossibility, but as an inevitability. She began to identify herself as the type of person who graduated from college. Orlando encouraged her to keep going. Granny, too, pressured her to finish her education.

When she first arrived at Berea, Wilma had been content to earn C's. After all, she thought, a C is average, and she was perfectly happy to be average in this new and different world. But, once she went back to school, average was no longer good enough for Wilma. She knew she could be remarkable — she wanted to be, for her daughter.

She also didn't like Orlando having a better GPA than her — she knew that she was just as smart as he was. So she began studying with dedication and purpose; she was soon earning A's on her report cards. She once complained that she got only 104 percent on a test. With the bonus points, she could have gotten 105.

When I was five, my mother graduated from college. I remember getting a new dress for the occasion — the first I'd owned that was that fancy. It had lace trim and a delicate flower print. My mother bought me a child-sized graduation cap and gown and let me walk with her in the processional. "We're graduating!" I told my family as we walked past them down the aisle.

I didn't know then how true that statement was. How by graduating with her degree, my mother changed both of our lives. How the value that she had come to place on education would seep into my core and carry me far beyond the hills of Appalachia. How her ability to better herself and her family would set me up for success. The day after the graduation ceremony, the local newspaper ran a picture of the two of us, my mother and me, standing side by side, eyes focused forward, graduating to the next phase of our lives.

CHAPTER 3

One hundred and thirty-two, one hundred and thirty-three, I silently counted as I walked, *one hundred and thirty-four . . .* I knew the number of steps to the public library in Berea by heart. We went there almost every day, my mother and I, ostensibly because it was air-conditioned. Our apartment was not, and the electric fans we set up to blow through the house provided little relief.

We walked to the library because we didn't have a car; even if we'd had a car my mother wouldn't be comfortable driving. She hadn't had her license that long, and driving still made her nervous. Perhaps that's because neither Granny nor Papaw ever had a license. The one time Papaw tried to drive a neighbor's car he ran it straight into a ditch. When Wilma was first learning to drive, she crashed right into a bridge.

Once we reached the library, I relaxed into the cool air. It was small and poorly lit;

fluorescent lights hummed and flickered. The air smelled like damp paper, and everything looked just a little green. Although it was not objectively impressive, the library was, to me, the best place on earth.

We spent the hottest part of the day there, reading and talking. As we left, the librarian, who knew us by name, offered to let me pick a kids' book from the free book pile. I had no trouble choosing one because I had already combed through the pile several times that week, ranking the books in my head. Books about dogs, cats, and farm animals went to the top of the pile. Books about science fiction and superheroes went to the bottom.

Even before I was in school, I spent my days learning with my mother. We explored the backyard and tried to identify the different types of bugs and plants that lived there. I loved the earthworms, and I made it a point to rescue each one we saw stranded on the sidewalk after it rained. We made our own play dough and experimented with mixing the colors together. Inevitably, the dough turned a shade of dingy brown from my overly exuberant squirts of food coloring. We caught box turtles along the road and built pens for them in the backyard. The turtles dug out, and we would search the neighborhood for signs of the tall flowers we had taped to their backs.

My mother built her life around teaching me. Although she now had a college degree, she wanted nothing more than to be a stay-at-home mom. Once, a college professor shook her paper at her, saying, "You have the rest of your life to be a mother. You only have now to be a college student."

My mother responded, "I only have right now to be the mother of this four-year-old."

Wilma didn't know any other way to be in the world. Most of the women she had seen growing up were stay-at-home moms. She didn't know what it looked like to do anything else. And she was good at being a mother, always finding creative activities and new adventures. She had majored in child development in college, which had given her a new skill set with which to nurture and teach me. Everything was a life lesson.

As I got older, this emphasis on education shifted into the classroom setting. It didn't take much for my mother to convince me that schoolwork was important: I had grown up watching her do her own, had spent my earliest days around classrooms and students. In my mind, getting an education was built into the backdrop of life, something you did because it was the only option, like breathing or sleeping.

It may not seem like much: a young girl enthusiastically embracing education, a mother emphasizing its importance. But this scene was the culmination of a story that began long before I was born.

When my mother was a child, Papaw never placed much of an emphasis on his children getting an education. Perhaps that was because he himself never went past elementary school. J.L., the oldest child, never finished middle school. Vernon, the second oldest, dropped out sometime around the third grade. Papaw didn't object, since he needed the extra hands to help out in the fields. Tobacco was the way — seemingly the only way — to support a family in Owsley County. Education was a luxury, thought Papaw, and a somewhat useless one at that.

The other children dropped out at some point during middle or high school, all for their own reasons. Ruth went sporadically as a child, and finally dropped out after her bout with rheumatic fever, one of the few times Wilma remembers seeing Ruth cry. She made her flash cards to study with in an attempt to cheer her up.

Dale dropped out because he was tired of

getting into fights. Some of the children teased him because he had only two shirts, which meant he wore the same thing several days in a row. Kids called him poor and dirty. Dale, feeling obligated to defend his family's honor, would fight them. After years of this, he was tired of getting in trouble. It was exhausting.

One by one, the first five children left school without a high school diploma. My mother and her siblings were not unique in this regard — most Owsley children didn't graduate from high school during this time. Aunt Ruth estimates that, in the 1960s, only one out of every five of her classmates finished school.

Even for those who did complete high school, attending college was virtually unheard of. Each year the valedictorian received a scholarship to enroll at Lees Junior College, a small campus one county over. Yet, inevitably, the student would return to Owsley County a few months later. "I missed my family," they would say. "I'm back here and I'm staying here."

So it was surprising when Granny, an elementary school dropout herself, started telling Wilma that she should go to college. "Get your degree," she said. "Make something of yourself." College was not something Granny was familiar with — I'm not sure she ever set foot on a college campus. It's strange that she decided she wanted to have a child who was a college graduate.

She'd said similar things to her other children over the years, but none of them had listened. All her kids respected Granny, but her voice was not the loudest in their lives. Four of her first five children were boys, and they spent most of their time in the fields with Papaw — that's what boys were expected to do. Ruth, who didn't like being singled out as the only girl, also preferred to work alongside her father. He was the model they wanted to grow up to emulate. It was a model that didn't call for extended education.

But Wilma, the younger daughter, was Granny's most reliable housework assistant. Wilma didn't mind cooking and cleaning and house chores, so she spent more of her time inside with Granny — especially in the off-season when there was less farmwork. Hearing Granny's repeated plea that she go to college stuck with Wilma. She began to think there was something to it.

Wilma had always liked school, and she had always been good at it. When she was a young child she desperately wanted a kids' encyclopedia set. Her parents couldn't afford to buy her one, so she schemed up a way to get one herself. She knew that there was a call-in radio show that let people submit questions. If your question was selected, you got an encyclopedia set as the prize. Wilma spent weeks pondering the right question before she finally sent one in. When she heard them read her question on the air, she squealed. She cherished that encyclopedia set, carefully hiding it from her rowdy brothers.

When Wilma was in middle school, she made friends with an older woman named Belle who lived at the top of the holler. Belle had noticed Wilma and her siblings walking up out of the holler each morning to wait for the school bus. Belle would lift the corner of her lace curtain and watch them jostle and joke with one another as they stood in the cold morning air. She invited the gaggle to wait inside. "You'll catch your death of cold!" she told them as she ushered them in.

Over time, a friendship developed. The children would fetch her eggs and sweep the house. Belle, in return, gave them jelly beans and helped out the family financially. Belle instinctively knew that Papaw was too proud to accept any offers of charity — he could take care of his own family, he said time and again. Instead, she paid him extra money to mow her lawn and gave the children hand-me-down shoes.

Belle's son, Bob, was a doctor. Most Owsley County residents didn't know anyone who had "made a doctor of himself," and they spoke of Dr. Bob with a sense of awe. After Dr. Bob graduated from medical school, he set up his practice in a larger town in Kentucky. But he would come back to Owsley County on the weekends to "doctor" to anyone who needed medical care, and he didn't charge for his services. Even though a lot of children in the area qualified for government health insurance, many parents were too proud to utilize it. Papaw and Granny were among these proud residents, so they took their children to Dr. Bob for care.

It was during one of these weekend visits that Dr. Bob met Wilma. "What makes a cut scab over?" she asked, her brows furrowed, as he disinfected her wound. He was impressed with her quick wit and insightful observations about the world. He knew immediately that someone should nurture her inborn ability. So he gave her books and helped her apply to summer camps for children from Appalachia. He encouraged her to be active in her local youth group, which planned occasional trips to other parts of the state.

I often wonder how things would have been different for the other members of my family if they had been lucky enough to have someone nurture their intelligence. Granny was one of the smartest women I've ever known. She could disassemble any electronic device — a television, a radio — into hundreds of pieces and figure out how to make it work again. She could do math, mostly related to recipes and household expenses, in her head with surprising speed and accuracy. She would use the tiniest inconsistency in a story to deduce what the person was lying about and why. With her logic skills, people skills, and penchant for drama, she would've been an excellent lawyer.

The same potential existed in Ruth. When Ruth was in her thirties, she worked doing odd jobs for a female preacher in a neighboring county. The preacher, after realizing Ruth hadn't graduated from high school, helped her enroll in a GED program. Ruth studied for just two weeks before taking the exam — she couldn't afford to spend any more time on it. Despite her limited formal education and short study time, Ruth scored in the seventieth percentile. To this day, she proudly displays her framed GED certificate on a wall in her house.

But my mother was the one who got lucky.

When Wilma told her family that she was going to apply to college, most of them didn't say much. Likely, they had no frame of reference from which to draw questions. How do you ask about a concept you know nothing about?

Only Ruth was encouraging. Even though Ruth was still young, she was already beginning to see the way that a life in the tobacco fields affected her body. She would have multiple skin cancers by her midthirties. She would cut them off herself with a pocketknife because she didn't have health insurance. She developed arthritis early in life. She wanted better for her younger sister.

She always had. Ruth had cared for Wilma from the time she was born. Granny was too busy to dote on every child, and Ruth — nine years older than Wilma — was often left in charge of her. When Wilma was a toddler, she developed a condition that made it hard for her to swallow. It was Ruth who made sure that she ate enough and took her medicine. "At first you was a fussy baby because you was sick," Ruth tells Wilma, "but then you was fussy just because you was spoilt. And I's the one that spoilt you."

One of Wilma's earliest memories is of Ruth babysitting her and her siblings while Granny and Papaw were away for the night. After it got dark, someone began to rattle the front door, trying to break into the home. Burglary wasn't unheard of in the hills, and there was a spot up the road from the farm where the local teens would hang out and "get up to no good," as Granny would say. Wilma, terrified, began to cry. Ruth, still a teenager herself, grabbed a loaded shotgun and stuck it out the window next to the door. "Rattle it again," she said, her voice deeper than normal. When the would-be intruder did, she fired the gun. She missed him, but nobody ever bothered the house after that.

When Ruth was young, she sometimes missed school because she didn't have sturdy enough shoes to walk the mile-plus out of the muddy holler. It seemed easier to stay at home than to show up with sore and dirt-covered feet. As a teenager, she remembered the embarrassment of those tattered, muddy shoes and vowed that things would be different for her younger siblings. So when it rained, Ruth would put Wilma and Charlie on a pony and lead them up to the top of the ridge to wait for the bus. She didn't want them to worry about their shoes while they were in school. She wanted them to be able to focus on learning.

Unlike Ruth and Granny, Papaw hated the idea of Wilma leaving for college. "What would you want to go away an' leave your family for?" he asked Wilma, genuinely not understanding her motivation. People in Owsley County stayed close to their families. Families took care of their children. Papaw couldn't fathom why Wilma would forgo the comfort and security that home offered her. "Please, Wilma," he begged, "just stay home and let me take care of you." He didn't seem to realize that if she stayed, she would be the one who would spend her life doing nothing but caring for others. He tried, time and again, to talk her out of going.

I sometimes wonder why the women in my family valued education more than the men did. Granny and Ruth craved education with their whole beings. Even when they couldn't have it for themselves, they wanted it for the other members — particularly the female members — of the family. But the men — Papaw, Vernon, even Dale — didn't seem to value it in the same way.

Maybe it's because they, as men, already had access to the few opportunities available in Owsley County. There wasn't much privilege to be had there, but where it existed it belonged to men. They could buy or rent a farm, be the heads of their families, participate in a more public life. Women, in contrast, were largely confined to the private sphere, to their homes. There weren't a lot of ways for them to take charge of their destinies. Maybe they saw education as one way that they could.

They weren't the only Kentucky women who believed that. In the late nineteenth and early twentieth centuries, some educational institutions — mostly in New England — began to open their doors to women. Many well-to-do Kentucky women, mostly from wealthy urban centers such as Lexington and Louisville, had the opportunity, for the first time, to go to college. Because education had been denied to them for so long, they understood that it had real power. They had fought, protested, argued, for the right to access higher education.

As this door opened for them, they felt compelled to use the opportunity to help open doors for others. Some came back to Kentucky to found settlement schools, which provided a free education to some Appalachian students well before there were public schools in the area. In a world with few career choices for educated women, settlement schools were a way for Kentucky women to make a difference in the male-dominated world that surrounded them. I like to picture them, these women, making their way through the mountains toward unknown people and possibilities. Not every child, not even the majority of children, got to attend a settlement school. But some did, and that was progress.

While Appalachian communities are often portrayed as patriarchal — and in many ways rightfully so — they also realized that the women running the settlement schools knew things that mountain people did not know, and that this new knowledge was important. By the 1930s, there were 200 settlement schools across the southern United States. Despite the prevalence of these institutions, Granny never had a chance to attend one. There wasn't one in Owsley County, and even if there had been, her family couldn't have spared her from the tobacco fields. Even in the communities that supported the settlement schools, there were certain realities that families had to contend with.

If Granny and Papaw ever fought about education, about whether they would support Wilma applying for college, they kept it a secret from their children. Granny had grown up believing that a wife didn't question her husband in front of his family. But I like to think that Granny, ever persistent, brought it up in the evenings, when the two of them had a few minutes of privacy in their own room. "She's going to college, and that's that," Granny would say, her jaw set in the way that let Papaw know she meant business. "You might not like it, but you's best keep yer mouth shut." Papaw, recognizing the tone in her voice, would nod his acceptance.

When Wilma began seriously considering college, she assumed that she would go to Lees Junior College like the few other students in Owsley County who made it on to higher education. She didn't know any kids who had gone anywhere else. But Dr. Bob had other ideas. He knew that if Wilma went to Lees she would live at home and commute. She would stay in her same environment, where education wasn't valued and other obligations were omnipresent. She would become another college dropout who ended up in debt and back on the farm.

"If you apply to Lees," Dr. Bob told Wilma, "I'll deny your application. I'm on the board. I can do that."

"But that's not fair!" Wilma cried. "I want to go to Lees."

"You're going to Berea," Dr. Bob replied. "It's a school where you can make something of yourself. It's where you need to be." Dr. Bob had gone to Berea. It's where he met his wife, and where his love of medicine was born. He had seen firsthand the power of the school to change lives. Wilma could tell by the tone of his voice that she wasn't going to change his mind.

Reluctantly, she agreed. She trusted Dr. Bob, and knew he had more knowledge about colleges than anyone else in her life. Plus, Wilma was a people pleaser by nature, and she didn't want to disappoint this man who had invested so much in her future. So she applied.

The day Wilma got her Berea acceptance letter, the family gathered around the kitchen table. Even though most of her older siblings, except Ruth, had moved out of the house, they still came back for dinners several nights a week. Granny was setting the corn bread on the table with a particularly proud look on her face. "Go ahead and tell them," she said, her eyes sparkling with excitement.

"I'm going to college," Wilma said hesitantly. "Berea College."

Ruth offered words of praise and encouragement. "I'm proud of you, sis," she said as she playfully punched her shoulder. But the others sat there, nodding a bit before moving on to the next topic of conversation. I wonder if my mother second-guessed herself in this moment. Did she worry that she would grow apart from her family? Be the only one not at the table for regular dinners? Leave the hard work to them, while she went to sit in a classroom?

The night before she left for college Wilma was crying as she packed up her few things. "I don't want to go," she told Ruth. "I don't know why I'm doing this." She flung another T-shirt into a worn duffel bag. Ruth walked across the room and put both hands on Wilma's shoulders. She looked her in the eye and firmly said, "You're going, Wilma. You have to go. You're going so you don't stay here and work as hard as I do. Go on and make something of yourself."

"But I don't even have any money for books." Wilma sobbed. "I can't go." A few hours before, Papaw had come into Wilma's room, his tall frame stooped with the weight of bad news. Money was tight, he said. The tobacco hadn't done as well last year. He didn't have any extra money to give her for books, one of the few things she needed money to purchase. Maybe the money shortage was real; maybe Papaw was trying desperately to stop his younger daughter from leaving home.

Ruth didn't hesitate. "I have your book money." She walked into the next room to a beat-up dresser. She reached inside and pulled out a gray sock with a red toe. In that sock was the money Ruth had earned mowing lawns, working in neighbors' tobacco fields, and doing other odd jobs around town. The small savings represented hours of back-breaking labor. She pulled out a handful of wrinkled bills and counted them quickly. She smoothed them once and handed them to Wilma. "I don't want to hear no more about it." She paused, then added with a half smile, "And if you don't go I'll beat the livin' tar out of you."

Wilma knew better than to protest. You didn't win arguments with Ruth. Wilma silently placed the well-worn bills — more than enough to cover the cost of books — into a zippered pocket of her bag. They both knew Ruth had just guaranteed her younger sister would have the future that Ruth had once wanted for herself.

Others helped Wilma as well. Dr. Bob and some neighbors gave her money to buy school supplies. Granny bought her a jumbo-sized bag of peanut M&M's. The community came together to support one of their own venturing off on a journey they didn't quite understand.

The next morning Ruth loaded up Wilma's belongings into their brother Vernon's pickup truck. Granny and Papaw waved from the porch as Wilma climbed into the vehicle. Papaw went back inside before Vernon started the engine, too emotional to watch his daughter drive off. Right before they set off from Cow Creek, Ruth hugged Wilma close and whispered: "Go on and get out of here. And don't be pinin' after this place. There won't be nothin' waitin' fer ya back here." Wilma took one last look at the farm, then set her gaze ahead as they began to drive away.

CHAPTER 4

Shortly after I was born Papaw began to get confused frequently. He would forget where he was and why he was there. Dates got jumbled up in his mind. It didn't take long for the doctor to diagnose him with Alzheimer's disease.

Granny insisted on caring for him at home. She was terrified of hospitals, convinced that they often killed patients. She had learned that fear from her mother when she was a child.

Granny's father worked part time at a sawmill. One day, he was walking his normal route through the mill when he saw some coal ash on the floor. Thinking nothing of it, he walked over it, not realizing that there were hot embers burning underneath. The heat melted his boots to his feet and left him with severe burns.

"You just need to let it heal up," the local doctor told him as he dressed the wounds.

71

The doctor gave him some ointment and some bandages and taught his family how to tend to the burns. Granny's mother believed she could give him all the care he needed at home, so he received no further treatment. She was distrustful of modern medicine, seeing it as something strange and incomprehensible, not a part of her traditional community.

Life became harder for Granny after her father's injury. She had to work longer hours in the field to make up for his absence. She had new chores to take on because he could no longer help on the farm. She and the rest of the family spent hours caring for him, changing his bandages, carrying him from room to room.

About a year after the accident, he died from infection. Granny was blunt when she described it to me: "His feet just rotted off and killed him." She said this calmly, matter-of-factly. Living in a community with no money, no healthcare, and few worker protections had taught her that accidents — even horrific ones — were a part of life.

This wasn't the first horrific accident she had seen. When she was young, Granny and her nine-year-old sister, Ruby, were standing near the fireplace that heated the drafty house. It was Christmas Day. Ruby was wearing long skirts, as she always did, because Granny's mother didn't believe that "girls had any place puttin' on britches." Ruby, young and a bit cold, stepped too close, and her skirts caught fire.

"Somebody grab her!" the family shouted as they tried to wrap the screaming child in blankets to smother the fire. But Ruby, in a panic, broke free of their grasp and sprinted out the door. She ran down the hill, fire and smoke billowing behind her. When she reached the creek at the bottom of the hill, she paused. With one final scream, she jumped into the icy water. They pulled her limp body out of the creek, skin and garments in tatters. She died a short time later.

The family went on after these deaths because they had to. They didn't have the luxury of allowing their grief to consume their lives. There were still too many mouths to feed and not enough resources to feed them. So they threw themselves into farmwork, using busyness and exhaustion to bury their grief. But they never forgot the family members they lost so tragically. When Granny was seventy years old, her blue eyes would still well with tears if someone mentioned her sister Ruby. "She was such a beautiful girl," she would say wistfully. Even though Granny accepted accidents, sickness, and death as a fact of life, her acceptance didn't erase her sorrow.

Caring for Papaw wasn't easy for Granny, but she tackled the task with her characteristic strength. Ruth helped too, but she was largely preoccupied keeping the farm afloat. Most of Papaw's caregiving fell to Granny, who fed him and bathed him and never once complained. But, even as a six-year-old, I could see that caring for him became harder for her over time. He needed constant attention, and it was increasingly difficult for her to leave him alone. One night at Cow Creek I woke up, sometime around three o'clock in the morning, and heard Granny pleading with Papaw from the front room. "Please, Willie," she said. "You're home. This is home. Please go back to sleep."

I'm sure Granny felt alone in these moments. She tried to put on a brave face, as she had always done, but there were cracks in her strong exterior. Occasionally I would wander into the kitchen and find her, one aged hand pressed against the kitchen table, the other squeezing the space at the top of her nose. Her eyes would have a vacant look, as though her mind were trying to escape itself, escape her body, for just a few minutes.

Still, her eyes held nothing but joy on the day Granny told me they were going to get a bathroom in the house. One of the neighbors knew Papaw was sick, and figured that an indoor toilet and bathtub would make it easier for Granny to care for him. The neighbor paid out of his own pocket for the addition.

At the time, I was just excited to have a toilet in the house. It was a clear, sunny day, and my cousins and I ran around the yard as the plumbers did their work. "No more outhouse, no more outhouse!" we shouted with the type of excitement that only children can muster about a bathroom. Every night we inspected the builders' progress, wondering out loud whether tomorrow might be the day when the work was complete.

Back then we didn't realize the true impact of this gift — how extraordinary it was that the neighbor had given it to Granny. It's only now that I see it in its full context, as another example of Owsley County residents taking care of one another. This neighbor knew Papaw, respected his work ethic and how he raised his family. He had experienced Granny's hospitality and kind smile. He wanted to do what he could to make this terrible disease easier for them. He didn't have much money himself, but people were more important than dollars in the bank. He had to trust that if he was ever in need, someone would do the same for him.

And he had good reason to trust his community. The norm in Owsley County was to be generous with your neighbors. Most families were one unlucky occurrence away from being hungry. Generosity was both an insurance policy and a deeply held value.

On the weekends, my mother and her siblings would do odd jobs at the stockyards to help make ends meet. Dale remembers working there, barefooted, when he was six years old. A community member felt bad for this child with muddy feet and too much responsibility, and gave him money to buy a pair of work boots. Six decades later, Dale's eyes get wide and his jaw firms up when he tells this story. He wants people to understand how deeply that act of kindness impacted him.

Even in their poverty Granny and Papaw taught the children to return the generosity that they so often benefited from. For Granny and Papaw, that took the form of growing an extra garden of food to give away to needy families in the community.

This meant added work, and the children used to complain about spending more time in the hot sun. "Why do we have to pick all those green beans?" Wilma once asked. "We've got plenty to get us through the winter."

"There are hungry chil'ren 'round here," Papaw told her, "and we're going to help feed them." Wilma and Papaw spent the rest of the day in the fields. Community was a thing to be worked for, nourished, valued.

Some say that this sense of community has eroded over time — that it has crumbled under the feet of the current generation. There may be some truth in that. Technology, our modern world, has changed the way we build and define community. We don't see one another in the same ways that we used to.

But the mountains are still full of people, often women, taking on quiet leadership roles to move their communities forward. One woman I know runs a community garden, where anyone in need can gather food for their family. Another started a program that gives out seeds and fertilizer at the beginning of the growing season so people can grow their own food. This strategy works well in the mountains, since many people remain too proud to accept anything they perceive as charity.

I talk sometimes with a friend who lives a few counties away from Owsley about community in Appalachia, about why individual people often take on the roles that government or nonprofits play in other communities. We muse that it's in part because each person is known in a small mountain town. Each person's suffering is personal, felt by others. It's hard to stand by when you see struggle with your own two eyes. It's also in part because institutions have failed to make things better. Over the years, many an outside organization has promised to improve life for people in the mountains. Some have delivered on their promises, but most have not. So people inside the communities take the resources they have and set to work.

Sometimes outsiders come in and want to save Appalachia. It's not a bad instinct — I can understand where it comes from. But outsiders who rush into the hills don't always take the time to see that mountain people are a creative, resourceful lot. They don't understand that Appalachians can be — should be — partners in the effort to make their lives better. They don't grasp that, if given the right resources and opportunities, these communities are capable of saving themselves. If there's one thing that women in these hills know how to do, it's get things done.

The change in Papaw's health led to other changes at Cow Creek. Papaw and his children had always farmed tobacco. Most of the small farms grew tobacco in those days for reasons closely tied to geography and politics. The rolling hills limited the size of most farms, and tobacco was one of the few crops a small farm could make enough money off of to survive.

At that time, the federal government controlled tobacco production through a quota system. Under this system, a farmer was limited to growing a certain quantity of tobacco each year. If the farmer couldn't sell his crop at market, the Burley Tobacco Growers Cooperative Association — a farmers' co-op that received some government support — promised to buy that farmer's tobacco at a set price. This, in effect, subsidized the tobacco grower and kept tobacco prices stable. Originally the goal of this system was efficiency: by guaranteeing tobacco farmers a high price, the government incentivized farmers to grow the much-demanded crop and provided security to small farmers.

Growing tobacco is labor intensive. The

first step is for the farmer to set the tobacco plants in the field. Once the plants reach near-maturity, he "tops" them: cutting off their tops to force them to grow out instead of up. This causes each plant to grow larger leaves, a benefit for commercial production. Usually topping is combined with spraying the plants with pesticides to protect them from insects.

A few weeks after topping and spraying, the farmer cuts down the tobacco and places several plants on a single stake. He then hangs these stakes in a barn where the tobacco can dry and cure. Months later, when the humidity is just right, he will remove it. Finding the right moment is crucial; if the air is too dry, the leaves will crumble and fall apart. Papaw would often wake up at two A.M. to remove the tobacco, waiting for the perfect pre-dawn humidity. Next, the farmer tears the leaves from the sticks and places them in bundles. He then transports these bundles to the market, where he sells them. Papaw always tried to sell his tobacco in November so that he would have enough money to buy each of his children an apple and two sticks of candy for Christmas.

Despite tobacco's continued profitability in the 1990s, the many steps in the growing process meant that my family could no longer afford to farm it. As Papaw's health got worse and the other siblings started families and lives of their own, it became harder for Aunt Ruth to find and pay for the help she needed. Eventually, she had to acknowledge defeat.

I'm sure that wasn't an easy thing for Ruth to do. She is a woman who gets things done, even when those things are difficult. She kept farming tobacco years after she should have because she believed that her willpower could hold the family together. But Ruth also has a pragmatic side, and one day, without tears or fanfare, she announced that she was done growing tobacco. She took a job working as a cashier at the Family Dollar in town, and the fields on Cow Creek sat empty.

It wouldn't be long before the rest of Eastern Kentucky would follow suit, but for different reasons. Over time, inefficiencies had entered the quota system. Each farmer had received his quota right as part of the 1930s New Deal reforms. Quota rights were handed down from generation to generation, and there was no mechanism for a new farmer to receive a quota of his own. Instead, if someone wished to start growing tobacco, he had to purchase land that already had a quota allotment or lease a quota from someone else.

Cultural attitudes toward tobacco shifted around the 1990s, and the public soon grew wary of government involvement in the tobacco industry. The added barriers to entry for new farmers — many who wished to start large tobacco farms — made the quota system unpopular with powerful people in the agriculture industry. The federal government eliminated the quota system in 2004; the change took effect in 2005.

The decision sent shock waves through the Eastern Kentucky mountains. Tobacco farms became larger, taking advantage of economies of scale and large farms' ability to bear the risk that comes with no price support. The small farmers folded fast. There were 93,330 tobacco farms in the United States in 1997. This number dropped to 56,879 just five years later. By 2015, only 4,268 tobacco farms remained. Tobacco is no longer a reliable way for small farmers in Appalachia to make a living.

Today Owsley County is full of vacant fields and desolate barns. Structures and places that used to be alive with sound, energy, and movement now rest idly in the mountain hollers. Nothing has come to fill the emptiness. Many programs across Kentucky have focused on providing new jobs and new skills to former tobacco farmers, but those programs have been unable to break into this particular place in the mountains.

Coal, too, is on the decline. There's not much coal in Owsley County — there never has been — but coal mining was prevalent in several nearby counties. Since 2011, the coal mining industry in Appalachia has lost 33,500 jobs. Even after Donald Trump carried coal country in the 2016 election by promising to put miners back to work, the number of coal jobs has continued to drop. And, unsurprisingly, a loss of mining jobs is associated with decreased incomes in many Appalachian counties.

Coal has a long, complicated history in the mountains. In the early 1900s, smooth-talking salesmen from outside the state came and purchased rights to land in Appalachia. People dispute the reason they were able to do this. Some say it's because many Appalachians didn't realize the value of the resources they were selling — of the timber on the land and the minerals underneath it. Proponents of this view claim mountain people sold these rights for a fraction of their true value because, in a culture where one's word is important, they assumed good intentions of the outsiders offering money.

The other side disputes the characterization of mountain people as naïve. As one former government official told me, "People knew what they were doing. They were smart." He pointed out that many Appalachians received multiple offers to buy their mineral rights, and they negotiated to ensure they received a fair price.

Regardless of why and how these outsiders were able to purchase these rights, they eventually began to mine the land. Over time, they bought additional land from small regional mines doing the same. This created a system where much of the wealth of Appalachia was owned by people who didn't live there. In the 1970s, Pike County, on the far eastern edge of Kentucky, had the highest concentration of millionaires in America. But few of these millionaires actually lived there. Instead, they listed the county as an address for business purposes.

When people live outside the community, they have little incentive to invest back into it. They don't send their children to the local schools, take their family to the local health clinic, or drive on the local roads.

Without this connection, profit can become more important than people. As one person put it, "They build wood houses for folks to live in instead of brick."

Those who were powerful in the mining business found ways to have a powerful influence over local government. They lobbied for policies that kept taxes on coal low, which meant local communities received less revenue. They fought against increased worker protections. To compete with the lower price of coal mined elsewhere, mine owners decreased the wages they paid to their employees rather than cut into their own profits. The living conditions of the miners and their families suffered.

The effects of this situation weren't as obvious when coal was doing well — there were plenty of jobs and people could still make a comparably decent living mining. Yet, over time, coal production began to decline. There are a lot of complicated reasons why, but most economists agree it had to do with competition from natural gas, growth in solar and wind production, and new environmental regulations. Whereas coal provided half of the nation's electricity in 2000, that number dropped to 30 percent by 2017.

Many argue that even if coal does make a

comeback, it won't benefit Appalachia. Coal is more expensive to mine here. That's because much of the coal that is easy to get to has already been mined, meaning that miners have to go deeper into the mountain to find a coal seam. In 2013, 68 percent of Kentucky coal came from underground mines and 32 percent came from surface mines. In 2018, the amount from underground mines rose to nearly 80 percent.

Mines in Appalachia are smaller than they are in many places out west, and the average miner produces less coal per hour. Whereas an underground coal miner in Appalachia can produce three tons of coal per hour, a strip miner in Wyoming can produce close to twenty-eight. Appalachian coal mines employ 56 percent of the coal workers but produce only 24 percent of the coal.

None of this is meant to minimize the hurt Appalachians feel over the decline of coal. Coal was tied to families, history, pride — and rightfully so. Even those who oppose the coal industry acknowledge the strength of its workers. For some families, coal mining was a way of life, a good-paying job passed down from generation to generation.

A lot of people in the mountains feel that coal and tobacco went away because of forces outside of their communities. That somehow politicians and power structures far from these mountains are to blame for the emptiness that now pervades them. There is a sense that people are suffering, and that they themselves did not do anything to deserve it. And often, when people talk about the void left by coal, they don't talk about what will come next to fill it.

When I am in Owsley County, I like to drive to the once vibrant tobacco fields on Cow Creek. In them, I see the image of Aunt Ruth, of countless others, bathed in sun and sweat. I remember the feeling of being covered in earth and full of exhaustion. The economies of the past aren't the way forward for Appalachia. Those are the jobs that injured Granny's father, broke Papaw's body, and stole a part of Ruth's youth. They are the jobs that have killed many coal miners and given countless others black lung disease. These communities deserved — continue to deserve — better. But when I think about the care and the effort that went into this land, I am hopeful: I know that that same drive, energy, and determination still exist here. If only there were a different way to use them.

CHAPTER 5

I rushed out of my fifth-grade classroom one afternoon, eager to find my mother in the school pickup line. All day I had been full of anticipation. I had to get to Owsley County as quickly as possible.

Aunt Ruth had a date.

Aunt Ruth had never dated before. Many times I had asked her, "Aunt Ruth, when are you going to get a boyfriend?" She acted surprised each and every time. She said that she had work to do. That Papaw didn't like it. That she was too busy for a boyfriend. She had a million excuses, and she would hand them out with a smile and a quick pivot in the conversation.

But things in Owsley County had changed, the type of change that was complete and disorienting. A couple of years before, Papaw had died from Alzheimer's-related complications. He had been sick for the better part of a decade, and his tall, work-hardened body finally gave out.

Granny buried him in his overalls. He always wore overalls, no matter the occasion. On my mother's wedding day, he showed up in his nicest pair of bibbed ones. Despite his happiness that his daughter was getting married, he refused to walk her down the aisle because he was ashamed he had nothing else to wear. My mother, upset that her father wouldn't give her away on her wedding day, begged him to change his mind. When he refused, she had her brother Dale walk her down the aisle in his place.

Papaw had such pride in public. He was a tall man who always stood straight and looked people in the eye. He stopped going to a store in town because the owner made a snide comment about his muddy clothes. Papaw fiercely defended his reputation if it was ever called into question.

Yet I think he also had a lot of private shame. Shame in the clothes he wore, the way he lived, his unshakable poverty. He worked twelve-hour-plus days on the farm to be able to provide for his family. I'm sure there was a part of him that felt guilty that he couldn't provide more. I think he knew some people in the world were asking why he couldn't do better. I hope, in the end, he found peace.

Papaw's death meant that Granny and Ruth were the only ones left at Cow Creek, living in a house that was rapidly falling apart. A chunk of the front porch had rotted out. The barn was increasingly unsound. There were neither the hours in the day nor the dollars in the bank to take care of everything.

For a while, they made it work. The previous landlords had set it up through a lawyer for Granny to have a life estate at the farm, meaning that she could stay, rent free, for the remainder of her life. The Reeds had bought the farm with that understanding — plus they weren't about to kick out a good family that had fallen on hard times. Finally, though, Aunt Ruth and Granny gave up the lease on Cow Creek. Ruth, never one to show too much emotion, cried the day they sold the farm animals.

The once family-filled home became vacant. With the tobacco industry in decline, nobody else wanted to rent it, and it would sit empty for decades. A few meth addicts looking for a place to cook drugs would be the only people to enter it for the next twenty years.

Dale owned a piece of land on the other side of Booneville, just up the hill from his house. He offered to let his mother and sister put a trailer on it. Ruth and Granny agreed. I went with them to buy that trailer. It had low ceilings and a narrow hallway. The walls were covered in cheap, fake wood paneling. No matter how much Granny cleaned it, it always felt just a little bit dirty. Dale built a wooden porch onto the front to make it feel more like a home.

This new home, however lackluster it might seem, represented a new life for Aunt Ruth. For the first time in a long time, maybe ever, she had free time. She didn't have to wake up before dawn to tend to the farm. She didn't have to stay up late into the night worrying about all of the things wrong in the old, drafty house. She worked a normal eight-hour workday as a cashier at the dollar store. Afterward, she went home to a reasonable number of chores.

I'm not sure if she intended to fill her free time with companionship. Aunt Ruth never struck me as the romantic type. She was usually dressed in blue jeans and T-shirts. I don't think she owned any makeup.

But she did keep a romance novel on the stand near her bed. My cousin Melissa and I found it once, and we squealed over the cover with the shirtless men and fawning women in low-cut dresses. Aunt Ruth also let me and Melissa put makeup, usually borrowed from our mothers' makeup drawers, on her anytime we wanted. We weren't great makeup artists — we once covered her brows to lashes in neon-green eye shadow — but she often looked pleased when she saw herself in the mirror afterward. I'm sure there was a part of her that craved attention, romance, companionship. I'm sure there's a part of every person that does.

Shortly after Aunt Ruth began working at the dollar store, a man named Sonny started to come in regularly. Every morning around ten o'clock he would stop by to purchase washing powder. As he checked out, he would take an extra-long time at the cash register — there was never any line to speak of — chatting with Ruth about her day and the goings-on in town. "Did you hear what Johnny said to Pat yesterday?" he'd say, laughing and slapping his leg. After fifteen minutes or so, he would take his washing powder and leave. He would return the next day for the same routine.

Eventually, folks around town started to put two and two together. Sonny was a divorcé who lived by himself. Both of his sons were grown and out of the house. Surely he had no need for all that washing powder — he must have an ulterior motive. News quickly spread that Sonny was courting Ruth.

At first, Ruth wasn't sure how she felt about being courted. When she heard, through the town gossip mill, that Sonny intended to call to ask her on a date, she took the phone off the hook overnight. But Sonny was persistent. He knew that Ruth got to work about eight o'clock every morning and that it would take her about ten minutes to drive from her trailer to work. He called the house right before she left, just as she put the phone back on the hook. She decided that she might as well give him a chance.

For their first date, they planned for Sonny to pick her up and drive her to the Dairy Queen in Beattyville. Beattyville, a county over from Owsley, was about a twenty-minute drive and the closest town with a decent restaurant selection; in addition to the Dairy Queen, there was a pizza place.

When I heard that Aunt Ruth was going to the Beattyville Dairy Queen with a man, I knew this was serious. I knew with equal force that I had to be there. I begged my mother to drive me down and let me spend the night with Aunt Ruth. Melissa felt the same way I did. This was the most exciting thing we could remember happening in our lives. My mother agreed to take me. She was also excited for Ruth, and I wonder if she felt relief that Ruth was finally able to experience some of the things she had given up by staying at Cow Creek.

Melissa and I made plans to meet up at Aunt Ruth's trailer and wait for her to arrive home. Dale was Melissa's father, so Melissa lived just down the hill from Ruth. She came up as soon as she had finished supper. At first we sat outside, pushing the porch swing back and forth with our toes. As it got dark, we decided to hide near the front porch. We figured this was our best chance to try to catch Ruth and Sonny "a-smoochin'."

As Melissa and I hid in the dark, we talked about the things young girls talk about. Friends, activities, boys. I remember this conversation distinctly, because it was the first time that I noticed a difference between our lives. I talked about the activities I was involved in — all of the moving pieces of my young life. Girl Scouts, soccer, a community theater play. I talked about my friends, the sleepovers we had, and how we went for ice cream after we won a softball game.

Melissa didn't have these things to talk about. She didn't do any activities. No Girl

Scouts, no arts or crafts, no sports. I'm not sure if that was because activities weren't available — likely many of them were not — or because no one had helped her get interested in them. And although Melissa had friends at school, she didn't get to spend time with them in the same way I spent time with mine. Her parents were protective, worried about her being out of their sight for too long. As early as the mid-1990s, people were beginning to worry about the drugs seeping into the mountains. Meth was becoming more common, and Melissa's parents decided the best way to guarantee her safety was to keep her at home with them.

Even if they hadn't been as protective, there wasn't a whole lot for Melissa and her friends to do. There was no roller-skating rink or ice cream parlor. There wasn't even a McDonald's to play at. Now that the farm — and its veritable horde of animals — was gone, there were a lot fewer ways to entertain ourselves in Booneville.

The difference in our experiences gave me pause, even then. Melissa was just like me. We were blood. Kin. We had grown up together on Cow Creek. She was the closest thing I had to a sister. I depended on her to be like me. I didn't like the feeling of not knowing what to talk to her about.

This pause lasted only a minute, a brief glimpse of a hairline crack in our relationship that would eventually open up into a fissure. But it didn't separate us yet. Soon we were back to plotting the way to catch Ruth and Sonny romancing, and all felt well with the world again.

Eventually a truck pulled in and two people got out. Sonny and Aunt Ruth made their way to the front porch, talking in slow, low whispers. They weren't touching, but they looked intimate, like they were sharing secrets with each other. I took a step closer to try to hear what they were saying. A twig snapped under my foot. Aunt Ruth's head spun toward our direction, and we burst into guilty giggles.

"Cassie? Melissa? Is that you down there? Git yourselves up here! I never seen the like! Spyin' on your aunt Ruth!" Her voice sounded angry, but we knew that she wasn't. Her eyes were soft. She was happy to see us. We spent the evening on the porch with Sonny and Ruth, asking them questions about their date and what Sonny's intentions were toward our aunt. Later that night, after Sonny had left, Aunt Ruth pulled out the couch bed in the living room and we all three crawled in and watched the ten o'clock news until we fell asleep.

A few months later, Sonny and Ruth announced that they were getting married. Aunt Ruth was in her forties. She had never had a serious boyfriend, and she was pleased with this unexpected turn life had taken. Just like my parents, neither Ruth nor Sonny saw any reason to wait. There's a certain practicality in the mountains. Once you decide you love someone, you might as well get on with living your lives together.

Melissa and I approved of the marriage. We liked Sonny. He was a self-taught home builder. Even without formal training, he could design and build pretty much any type of house. He took us to a beautiful log cabin on the other side of Booneville that he had created all on his own.

In his free time, Sonny bought junked-out old cars and repaired them. Once they were finished, he showed them at car shows before selling them for some extra money. At that time, he had an old Chevy Nova that he painted candy-apple red. We took it to car shows, where we would set up lawn chairs and occasionally meander through the rows of vehicles. Afterward, Sonny would take us hot-rodding. Really, he just revved the engine a couple of times at a few stoplights. But we found it glamorous and exciting.

Shortly after they got engaged, Ruth went over to Sonny's house for a serious conversation. "Sonny," she said, "I just want you to know that if you ever put your hands on me in anger, I'll have to kill you." Sonny's eyes grew wide. "I might have to wait till you go to sleep one night, but I sure to God will stick a claw hammer in the back of your head." Sonny quickly assured her that she had nothing to worry about. But domestic violence was — and still is — common in Owsley County, and Aunt Ruth was glad that they had that conversation. At least if she had to kill him, she thought, she would've given him fair warning.

Ruth and Sonny planned the wedding quickly. Neither of them wanted much fuss, so they had a Friday-afternoon ceremony at the church they attended together. Aunt Ruth wore a modest white dress. My mother, Granny, and other family members made up the majority of the limited guests. I wasn't able to attend — I had a test that neither my mother nor Aunt Ruth would hear of me missing — but I insisted my mother recount every detail to me afterward.

At the time, Aunt Ruth's marriage stood out to me because of the marked shift it represented in my world. Aunt Ruth was independent. Aunt Ruth could do anything. She was strong in every sense of the word. And even at that age I knew that some men didn't like that — they liked their women to have some weakness in them. There was no weakness in Aunt Ruth.

Now that I'm older, Aunt Ruth's marriage stands out to me for similar reasons. Ruth got married at an older age in a culture where women got married incredibly young. She lived the first half of her life independently. It was very different from the experience of most women in the mountains.

It was very different from the experience of her mother.

Granny, whose given name was Emma Golden, met Willie, the man who would become my Papaw, in 1948. Willie was a kind man with a soft spot for animals and children. He used to carry around a kitten in the front of his bibbed overalls. If he forgot to pick up the kitten in the barn, it would chase him out into the yard. When he stopped, it would crawl into the leg of the overalls and scamper up toward Willie's pocket. He would grin as he fished it out and tucked it into the front pocket where it belonged. "Just hang tight, little buddy," he would say. "Just hang tight."

When they met, Emma was fifteen and Willie was thirty-two. No one was surprised when he started courting her. This age difference was common in marriages at the time, and tied closely to the local economy.

Most families in Owsley County made a living farming. In this environment, sons were a benefit; they were strong workers and could tend to the crops and animals. Sons might even be able to earn extra money by working in the fields of friends and neighbors. They also carried on the family name, which mattered in a place where your last name was a large part of your identity.

But daughters were a liability. The community saw women as less efficient, weaker, and more delicate than their male counterparts. It didn't matter that women were often the first awake and the last to bed at night. It didn't matter that they did both housework and fieldwork, all while birthing and raising children. Society had deemed women inferior workers. It was unlikely that another farmer would hire a female to help out, reducing the family's chance of added income from outside work.

My mother still remembers her father bickering with a neighbor after she and her brothers had spent the day working in his fields. The family had been topping tobacco in the hot July sun. At the end of the day, the neighbor, tallying up the amount he owed the family, informed Papaw, "I'm not paying for your daughter's work."

Papaw responded firmly, "She worked as hard as my sons. You will pay her the same for her labor as you pay them." His voice was calm, but his jaw was clenched.

But Papaw wasn't always so egalitarian in his views. In her twenties, Ruth gained a reputation for being one of the best tobacco workers in the county. Several farmers offered to pay her to work in their fields. But Papaw wouldn't let her go unless he accompanied her. It "didn't look right," he said, for his young, unmarried daughter to be unsupervised in the field with the men. Ruth sometimes turned down chances to earn money because Papaw couldn't go with her.

It was common in those days for sons to stay with their families well into their thirties before they began looking for a partner and an independent life. Most families tried to hold on to their boys as long as possible. Legend has it that Papaw's mother wept for months when his twin brother got married and moved to a farm of his own.

But families tried to marry off their

daughters as early as possible; sending a daughter away meant one less mouth to feed. It wasn't unusual for a girl as young as thirteen or fourteen to marry. A girl who reached the age of twenty without a husband was frequently referred to as an old maid.

Marrying girls off at a young age had an added benefit: It ensured that unwed daughters couldn't end up "in the family way." Back then, an unmarried pregnant daughter was a crisis for the whole family. Some families would turn pregnant daughters out of their homes, refusing to house the girls they felt had brought them shame. In rare circumstances, this still happens today. Aunt Ruth recently told me about a girl who became pregnant a few years ago, when she was just thirteen. Her family kicked her out. "I suppose some neighbor took her in," Aunt Ruth said. "I never did hear how she got by."

I used to assume that these actions were somehow grounded in religion — in a context of sin and casting it out. But Aunt Ruth says that they were often rooted in pride. "Truth be told, there weren't even that many churches 'round here in those days," she told me. "No, it didn't have nothin' to do with the churches. That was all pride is all that was." Hill people may not have much, but they have their pride. And if anyone — even a daughter — wounded that pride, the consequences could be severe.

Back in the late 1940s, Granny's family was thrilled by the potential match with Willie. Willie was an honest man from an honest family. He didn't have any money, but he was known as a hard worker. He rented a farmhouse, and he owned a bed to go in it. He could provide for their Emma, they thought.

Granny always said that she and Willie fell in love at first sight. He had come to her house on some other business when he saw her standing in the yard. It was springtime, and her yard was blooming with mountain wildflowers. Blues, yellows, and reds blended together in a bright montage. Willie thought Emma was the prettiest wildflower in the Appalachian Mountains. Within ten minutes they were sitting on the porch, giggling as they got to know each other.

Emma and Willie courted for two months before they got married. As was common in those days, they were supervised the entire time. The day Emma agreed to marry him, they had their very first unsupervised outing: to the courthouse to pick up the marriage license.

"Willie, I'm just 'bout the happiest girl in the world," she said as they walked into the courthouse to get the paperwork. Willie, never much of a talker, just smiled and held her hand a little tighter. They continued holding hands as they walked home, Emma's chatter breaking the silence of the surrounding mountains.

A few days later, the local preacher married them in Emma's living room. Emma got her first store-bought, or "brought-in," dress for the occasion. Years later, she smiled as she described the dress's shade of blue. "Like the summer sky," she said. She also told me she wore her house slippers that day. I'm not sure if that was because it was cold or because her only other shoes were work boots.

I struggle with this branch of my family tree. How do I reconcile the grandmother and grandfather I saw have a happy marriage with the little girl and the grown man sitting on the porch that day? Emma was a fifteen-year-old child. In today's world she wouldn't be allowed to drive a car or see an R-rated movie. Willie could be jailed for having a relationship with Emma. He had experienced two decades more of life than she had. How could these two people fall in love? In genuine love that was based on consent, compatibility, informed decision-making? It makes my gut churn to think of this girl, who never had a childhood, married at such a young age to a man who was so much older.

But I also saw this pair together in the later years of their life. Papaw would whisper sweet things to Granny that would make her blush like the young girl she was when they met. When Papaw's Alzheimer's disease advanced, Granny spent every minute caring for him with love and patience. Though he forgot everyone else, including his children and his siblings, he never forgot Emma, his mountain wildflower. I'm not sure I'll ever be able to satisfactorily square the gentleness, kindness, and love I saw between them with what I believe to be right and just.

I wonder if Granny thought about Papaw on Ruth's wedding day. I think she probably did. Granny was racked with grief after Papaw's passing. So much so that she stopped eating and sleeping. She wore her grief wrapped tightly around herself for years. I'm sure that, on Ruth's day of celebration, Granny was remembering the love and the family she and Papaw had built in Cow Creek.

CHAPTER 6

I was fourteen when my parents and I went to New York City. I had a track meet vaguely in that direction, and we decided that we should drive the rest of the way to spend a few days in the big city. We laughed and talked as the miles rolled past.

But once we hit New York we fell silent. There were too many cars moving too quickly. My dad hunched over the wheel, shoulders about his ears, glancing every so often at the directions he had printed off before we left. I could tell my mother was afraid: her hand gripped the handle of the door until her knuckles turned white. They both flinched when the first of several cab drivers honked at us. We were going at least ten miles per hour slower than any of the other vehicles.

The traffic was just the start — there were lots of things about New York that we found strange. The buildings were too tall and too close together. It felt like the sunlight could barely make it through to the street below. The people on the sidewalks didn't say hello to each other. They looked straight ahead, focused on nothing in particular and certainly not on one another. They didn't even smile as they passed.

I consider this trip to New York our first real family vacation. Sure, we had taken trips together before — including several camping excursions and a visit to Florida to see my dad's brother — but this time felt different. We had a hotel room in Manhattan. Yes, it had a bed that folded out of the wall, but it was a hotel in Manhattan nonetheless. We ate at restaurants, albeit affordable ones, every night. We weren't staying with relatives, and we didn't know a single person in the city. My parents' efforts to get an education, it seemed, had paid off.

My father, Orlando, had finished his doctorate in agricultural economics. After some time working as a postdoctoral assistant, he had landed a staff job at the University of Kentucky as an economist in the College of Agriculture. My father grew up on a farm, and he was interested in the ways that farming was changing in Kentucky. It had taken him a while to get to this place — having a wife and a child had slowed down the graduate-school process — but he had finally landed a secure position in an academic institution doing work that he loved.

My mother, too, was growing professionally. She had stayed at home with me for years, working part-time jobs or providing childcare in her home so she could focus on being a mother. But as I entered my teenage years, she decided to launch a career. She went into sales, working for a company that provided insurance to educators. She was immediately successful at it. People trusted her, and rightfully so. She would tell them if the plans she offered weren't right for them. "Well, I understand if you want to go with the other company," she would say. "I honestly think that's probably a better fit for you." She asked a lot of questions, both about people's insurance needs and about their lives. My father teased that her office was "one of the best places to socialize in town."

Beginning a career relit a spark inside my mother, the same spark that Berea College had kindled in her years before. Insurance agents take a series of tests to be able to sell securities and other financial products. The tests are difficult, and it's not uncommon for people to fail them several times. My mother decided that not only was she going to pass the tests, but she was going to ace them. She spent all summer studying on our back porch in the evenings. She and I would sit side by side in lawn chairs, scanning our books until the sky turned pink and the sun set. "I missed three questions on that last one," she said with disappointment one night after passing one of the tests. "I'll do better on the next one." We returned to studying in comfortable silence. She would go on to pass every test on her first try.

I'm sure we stood out terribly in New York — this family from the foothills of the Appalachians. It was summertime, and we wore bright T-shirts and jean shorts, in stark contrast to the sea of dark suits and neutral-toned dresses. I'm almost certain my mother wore a fanny pack — she had on almost all of our other family getaways. My mother's accent had grown fainter over the years, but you could still hear its lilt when she was nervous. And she was nervous most of the time we were in New York. "Do you think this neighborhood is safe?" she asked my father every time we went somewhere new. She kept checking her pockets to make sure nobody had stolen anything.

A few months ago, I was in New York for a friend's engagement party. Standing in line to buy a ticket for the subway, I remembered my parents standing in that same line at that same station years before. A man behind my father yelled angrily into his flip phone about "fucking tourists" as my father struggled to figure out how the ticket machine worked. My father's face turned a shade of red that matched his hair. I had never heard anyone say the word *fuck* in person before. It felt scary, but also a little exciting.

Once we were on the train we looked around at all of the other passengers. I've since learned that there is a code on the subway: Don't look directly at anyone. In a city with little physical privacy, anonymity is important. But, back then, I stared long and hard at each person I saw. My heart broke when a homeless man got on. I gave him one of the few dollars in my pocket as he passed by.

I thought about this family trip as I sat on the subway years later, looking at nothing and no one. Maybe it sounds cliché, but that first trip to New York has stuck with me. Not necessarily because of how uncomfortable I felt, but because of the current of possibility running underneath the discomfort. There was something invigorating about surviving three days in this strange and vibrant place — about seeing in person the things I had seen only in movies. It was challenging and endlessly interesting. To put it in terms my teenage brain probably thought in at the time, it felt very cool.

I had always loved adventure — seeing new places, doing new things. I think this started when I was a child on the farm. Granny, Aunt Ruth, my mother — they all allowed me to explore whatever environment I found myself in. I could roam the farm at will, climbing any tree, darting into any animal pen. They didn't hover or worry that I would hurt myself. They expected that I probably *would* hurt myself at some point, but they knew that whatever lesson I learned along the way would be worth the pain. They didn't want me to be scared of the world around me.

My cousin Melissa had started off the same way, but she was different by the time the New York trip came along. When we were younger, she would sometimes come up to Berea to stay a week with us. Even though Berea is a small town — with a population of around 15,000 people today — to her, Berea felt like a city vacation. We would go to the city pool and get Happy

Meals from the McDonald's drive-through. These were things not available to Melissa in Owsley County, and it was obvious that she relished them. She would call her parents every night and recount the details of each day, down to what we ate for dinner. She was particularly excited to report the night when my father had cooked. She hadn't seen a man prepare an entire meal for his family before. She still says that baked chicken was the best meal she's ever eaten.

But as Melissa got older, it was harder for her to stay away from home. Not because it was actually harder; we still invited her every summer and she still lived less than fifty miles away. But for some reason it felt harder to her. She didn't want to leave her home. She didn't want to be away from her parents. Her connection to Owsley County became stronger, and she wasn't interested in making connections anywhere else.

I'm not sure why this happened, but I suspect it might have something to do with fear. There's a narrative that people in Owsley County tell one another: The world is different outside of the mountains, and scary things happen there. To this day, Aunt Ruth still asks me about every shooting that happens in the city I live in. "Did you know that man that got shot?" she will inquire, and I will explain, once again, that there are hundreds of thousands of people where I live. But to her, it is all the outside, and it is all unnerving. I think that, as Melissa got older, she began to believe this narrative. Once she did, the excitement of adventure didn't outweigh the potential consequences.

But for me, at that time, adventure was still in fashion, and my trip to New York only reinforced my interest in exploring. The thought of New York, of what it stood for, stayed with me long after we got back to Berea. I suddenly saw Berea's location at the foothills of the Appalachians as symbolic: I was positioned at the edge of the mountains. I was at the gateway to the rest of the world.

It wasn't just that we had money to take a trip to New York. In everyday life, we could go to the movies and occasionally eat out at a sit-down restaurant. We went to the Olive Garden for special occasions like birthdays or my parents' anniversary. My mother took me back-to-school shopping at a mall in a nearby city. Over time, these things became a part of our new normal.

One of the first decisions my parents made with their new economic stability was to purchase a home. Up to that point, we had lived in various rentals: apartments, trailers, small houses. Once, my parents moved twice in the same week because my mother was afraid of the crowd hanging around the new apartment complex. The other tenants made too much noise and stayed up too late drinking. The landlord kept coming to check on my mother when she was home alone in a way that made her nervous about his intentions. My parents loaded up and moved on to the next place.

For years my parents had been searching for a house of their own. I think they probably began looking well before it was realistic to buy one. On Sundays, we would drive around Berea looking to find FOR SALE signs in the neighborhoods we liked. It was a fun game to play: What would it be like to live in that house? How great would my bedroom be if we lived in that neighborhood? Would I finally be able to get a dog if we moved to that place?

When I was ten, we found the brick ranch that would become our home. We all fell in love with it as soon as we saw it. My father walked through the house exclaiming "Wow!" each time he opened a door. The house wasn't large — around 1,700 square feet — but it was new. It was well built, and it had a backyard big enough for a dog pen. It had three bedrooms, and it was in a quiet neighborhood. My mother was giddy at the prospect of living in such a place.

My parents hemmed and hawed over whether they could afford it. The mortgage payment would be more per month than our entire family income when I was first born. Just like so many families who have struggled, they felt they couldn't entirely trust their newfound stability. They changed their minds several times over the course of the weekend. Finally, they decided to make an offer. The owner accepted it, and we moved in.

At the time, I didn't realize what a big deal it was, homeownership. But study after study shows the ways that homeownership positively impacts families. In 2013, the average net worth of a family who owned a home was $195,400, compared to $5,400 for those who rented. Net worth matters because it's a good snapshot of a person's financial situation.

Homeownership is associated with social benefits too. All other things being equal, children of homeowners do better in school, are more civically engaged, and are less likely to do drugs. That's not to say that homeownership is some magic fix to social problems. But it is to say that when my parents bought that house, they probably provided me with advantages beyond simply a bigger space to play in.

We celebrated my mother's thirty-first birthday shortly after we moved in. My father and I got an ice-cream cake and bought paper party hats. I got to bring my recently acquired puppy inside for the occasion. We had a lot to celebrate that year: new jobs, new house, new way of life.

What strikes me about this scene is the way it feels slightly backward. The way the events feel out of order, like a calendar that has the pages shuffled. There is a desired sequence to the major moments in life, a step-by-step process that we are told to follow: start a career, get married, buy a house, have a baby. My parents jumbled the order: get married, have a child, start a career, buy a house.

Their sequence of events certainly presented many challenges for them. Maybe it even presented challenges for me. But as I look back on my childhood, I realize that it also gave me the opportunity to watch my parents grow up. To see that special mix of pride and worry when the realtor told my parents the house was theirs; to watch my mother start a job and work hard to turn it into a career; to see my father finally be able to support his family in the way he had hoped to.

Not every couple who gets married so young and so poor finds their way to a happy ending. Couples who marry as teenagers, as my mother was on her wedding day, have a much higher rate of divorce. And college students with dependent children drop out of school at a higher rate than those without dependent children; only a third obtain a degree or certificate within six years. The odds were stacked against my parents. But through a mixture of support, hard work, and a little bit of luck, they were able to beat these odds.

Nowadays I tease my parents about getting married so young. "What were you all thinking?" I'll exclaim from time to time. "You had no business getting married and having a child! You were children yourselves!"

Inevitably, they will look first at each other, then at me, and smile. "But we were in love. And you turned out okay." Part of me is annoyed by their naïveté. I'm not sure they understand how different their lives could have, maybe even should have, been. But another part of me admires their unshakable positivity. I sometimes wonder if their sunshiny outlook is a whitewash, purposely bleaching away memories of darker, more trying times.

Around this time, Granny began to get sick. A few years before, a local doctor had seen what he thought was a spot on her lungs during a scan. Granny had been a heavy smoker for most of her life. Some of my earliest memories are of her sitting on the front porch at Cow Creek, her wrinkled hands holding a cigarette as she laughed. She quit smoking when I was four or five years old, after my mother threatened to stop letting me spend so much time in Owsley County if Granny didn't give it up. Granny stopped cold turkey.

Nobody was terribly surprised when they first heard news of the scan and its ominous spot. We all knew the health dangers associated with smoking — Granny did as well. It seemed almost predictable that she would suffer some sort of health consequences for her decisions. We knew the pattern of events.

Then something strange happened. Granny went to see a specialist at a rural hospital for a follow-up. That doctor did another set of scans and came back with wonderful news: The suspicious spot was gone. Granny was healed.

At the time, we all celebrated it as an answered prayer. News travels fast in Owsley County, and the whole community had been praying for Granny. Everyone took this as evidence that God himself had reached down to erase the spot on her lungs. I remember my Sunday-school teacher, a family friend who knew of Granny's illness, telling me how lucky I was that God had given my family this miracle. I said an extra set of prayers that night.

Now, though, I wonder if it really was a miracle or if the doctor had simply missed the cancer growing inside her. A few years later the cancer was back. And it was back in a way that looked as though it had never left — like it had been growing and spreading inside of her while we all celebrated her health.

Granny tried to put on a brave face when I asked her about it. I wasn't quite sure what to say, how to politely ask about being diagnosed with advanced lung cancer. Granny smiled and gave a laugh: "It'll take more than a little spot on my lungs to git your old Granny, don't you know it?" But I could see her lip quivering slightly. Her thick glasses magnified the extra moisture welling in her eyes. I knew that she was afraid. I was too.

The family — my parents, Ruth, Dale — encouraged Granny to come and stay with us in Berea while she got treatment. There was no place for her to get the radiation she needed in Owsley County. Things had come a long way over the years; there were now a couple of doctors who practiced in Booneville. But the type of specialized medical care Granny needed was not available in her mountain holler. And Granny had no way of driving herself to any out-of-town doctor's appointments. She never did get a license, and if there were programs to provide her with transportation to travel such a long distance on such a regular basis, she never heard of them.

Granny's situation mirrors that of Appalachia as a whole. Even today, the supply of primary care physicians is 12 percent lower in Appalachia than in the rest of the United States. This disparity is even greater for specialty care, at 28 percent. Focus in on rural Appalachia, and the supply of primary care physicians is 20 percent lower than in urban Appalachian areas, and the supply of specialists is 57 percent lower. Finding a doctor, particularly a specialist, is hard in Granny's part of the country.

That's why we were all thrilled to find out that a hospital in Berea had just purchased the type of technology Granny needed. My mother had flexibility in her insurance job, and she would be able to drive Granny to and from her doctor's appointments. It made sense that Granny would come and stay with us.

It made sense, that is, to everyone but Granny.

Granny let us all know that she didn't like the idea. "Lord, y'all just expect me to up and leave my home?" she protested, her voice shrill and alarmed. Home was everything to Granny. After Aunt Ruth married Sonny, Granny had moved to a semi-assisted living facility close to Booneville. She had a small apartment with new appliances and good lighting. It was a world above the falling-in particleboard trailer she had lived in for so many years. Although the facility didn't have the resources to drive her all the way to Berea for doctor's appointments, it could take her places like the local pharmacy and grocery store.

But most important, Granny had made friends. Her facility had a community room that she could walk to in the afternoons. A local preacher came a couple of times a week to hold a church service there. There were sometimes group activities or holiday celebrations. Granny took up crafting. It was the least isolated she had ever been. She had spent years living in a holler with no transportation, seeing her friends sporadically, if at all. Now she was steps away from company and companionship.

Granny embraced her new community and its members. Even when she was sick — on around-the-clock oxygen — she would drag her tank next door to help her friend Opsie wash her hair. She would weed her neighbor Claire's flower bed, scooting around on a board with wheels when she was too weak to stand. She swept her tiny apartment every day — often sitting in a chair — to make sure she was always ready for company.

There was something beautiful about this community full of aging mountain women. They had spent their lives surrounded by children and family, but perhaps lonely for friendship. Now they finally had a chance to sit, rest, talk. Many of them hadn't had time to visit with one another since they were children together so many decades before. It's no wonder Granny didn't want to leave.

As a compromise, my mother drove Granny back and forth from Berea to Owsley County a few times a week. The first day or so Granny was in Berea she would be happy to see us, telling us all about the goings-on in Booneville. "They killed Boogerman Peters!" she told us in horror. Strange nicknames were common in Owsley County; I know a Froggie, a PloughBoy, and a Digger. But this name sounded stranger than normal. When I asked her how this man — tragically murdered — had come to earn his title, she looked at me pensively. "Well, I suppose he kind of looked like a Boogerman," she replied after a few moments. I wasn't sure if I was supposed to laugh.

Inevitably, though, Granny wanted to go home. After being in Berea for a few days, she would come to my mother and beg, "Please, Wilma. I want to go home. Take me home." My mother would try to persuade Granny otherwise. Granny was getting sicker, her body weakened by the cancer and the treatment, and we were starting to worry about her living on her own. She had to drag her oxygen tank with her everywhere she went. But my mother was no match for Granny's persistence. Eventually we would load up the car and drive to Owsley County.

I sometimes think about all the iterations of women in my family who have traveled the curved road from Owsley County to Berea and back. From Wilma that first time on her way to college, to Granny and Wilma driving Granny back to the comfort of the mountains all those years later. That first journey opened up the path to Berea, but this didn't make it the destination for every woman who traveled it. Berea would never be home for Granny, nor for Ruth. In the same way, the road back to Owsley County was always open to Wilma. Yet it was never again her way home.

I wish I could say that having Granny with us more was always a joy, that I responded to the change in my teenage life with nothing but kindness and understanding. But this would be a lie.

There were times when it was wonderful, like when we went to the London flea market and Granny bought me my first Ralph Stanley cassette tape. We listened to it all the way home, my mother and I singing at the tops of our lungs. Granny sang too, her voice as loud and joyful as her weakened lungs would permit. My mother took us through a KFC drive-through, and we embarrassed her no end by cranking up the bluegrass music and dancing vigorously as the restaurant worker handed us our bucket of chicken. I can still picture Granny, too weak to move much, rolling her fists rapidly to the music, like a boxer hitting a teeny-tiny punching bag.

There was also the time Granny went to a bookstore with my mother and me. My mother was looking for some sort of professional book, and she left Granny and me to our own devices. Granny and I grabbed a cart and filled it with the most lustful-looking romance novels we could find. We brought the cart to my mother and asked her to buy its contents for us. My mother turned a bright red and exclaimed, "Good night! You two are trouble." Granny and I laughed all the way home. The next year for Christmas, Granny got me a romance novel.

Granny reminded us of the importance of family, of spending time with one another. One evening, my father wanted to watch a University of Kentucky basketball game in the living room. My mother, uninterested in sports, tried to convince Granny to go and watch a movie with her in a different room. Granny, a serious look in her eye, scolded her, "Orlando has been at work all day. I'm goin' to sit right here and spend time with him. I reckon you best do the same." Granny and Wilma joined Orlando to watch the game. Granny didn't know anything about basketball, but she cheered enthusiastically. It was a particularly physical game; at one point she jumped from her seat and shouted with venom, "You ain't nothin' but a big bully — take your tail end home!" My parents looked at each other in shock.

Granny also remained incredibly generous, just as she always had been. She survived off of nothing more than the small Social Security check she received each month, but she shared what little she did have. She took homegrown tomatoes to her pulmonary doctor's office because he had once mentioned that he liked them.

I, in particular, was the beneficiary of Granny's generosity. Granny always had a soft spot for her grandchildren, and she and I had a special bond. We both loved music, loved to dance. We liked getting out of the house, even if it was just to drive through town to see if we met anyone we knew.

When I was in high school, I started to learn how to play the guitar. Granny insisted on buying my first instrument. She would joyfully listen to me bobble chords, hearing the familiar songs I hadn't quite been able to bring into being yet. She would clap her hands to the errant beat, humming along to the twisted melody.

As my skills improved, Granny continued to buy me guitars. Every so often, when I was in Owsley County, she would ask me to come into her bedroom, claiming she needed my help with something. She would press a finger to her lips before reaching under her mattress, into a coat, or inside an old purse to pull out a couple of hundred-dollar bills. Granny didn't trust banks, and it was always interesting to see where she was hiding her money in any given week. She would whisper into my ear, "Go on and git you a new git-tar with this," before loudly asking me to help her move a chair from her bedroom to the living room. She knew my mother would scold us both if she caught Granny giving me so much money.

Granny got joy out of these gifts she could not afford to give. She had medical expenses, a fixed income. She must've been worried about having enough money to live on. Still, she gladly set aside large sums to buy me an instrument. All she asked in return was that I occasionally play a song for her.

I loved Granny. Full stop. No exceptions. But I am ashamed now that there were also times when I felt embarrassed by her. By her heavy accent and slow speech. By her unfailing, sometimes childlike, happiness. By her simplicity.

Once, when she was very sick, she came

to one of my soccer games. She and my mother set up folding chairs on the sideline with the other families. Granny spent the game yelling "Yay, Cassie!" each time I ran past her. Her fists were in the air and her eyes were sparkling. She was so joyful, watching her granddaughter play a mediocre soccer game. But I didn't relish her joy: I wanted her to be quiet. Her accent stood out and cut through the rest of the cheers. She had never been to a soccer game before, and she kept hollering at all the wrong times. At the end of the game, I intentionally walked off of the field in a direction that let me avoid saying hello.

I was becoming aware of the ways in which parts of my family were different. Different from the families on television. Different from the people in New York. Different, even, from many of the people in Berea.

I had always known the word *hillbilly*. I had heard Sonny, Dale, and Ruth use it often to describe themselves. "I'm just an old hillbilly — what do I know?" Dale would sometimes add after offering his opinion on something.

I understood that the word applied to people like Granny, my mother, maybe me. But I hadn't always known that I should be ashamed to be a hillbilly. I hadn't realized the way the rest of the world used that label as a brand. As a way to mark the inferiority of the people who live in the hills. As shorthand for all of the negative things the outside world thought about us: ignorant, lazy, unsophisticated.

I knew people who embodied some pieces of the hillbilly stereotype. Kin and acquaintances who didn't work, didn't travel, didn't trust the outside world. I have one distant cousin who had never left the state of Kentucky until a few years ago. One day, he went to Ohio for work, and called his mother from a friend's cellphone as he crossed the state line. "Mommy?" he said. "This is Elmer. This here O-hi-o looks like someone ironed out the land!" When I heard this story, I recognized that the rest of the world would laugh at him for fitting so easily into their idea of what a hillbilly is.

Even back then, I understood that hill people were more complex than the outside world believed. My family members were hardworking, quick-witted, and creative. The hill women I knew were strong and powerful. But still, the hillbilly label weighed heavily on me. One day at school, one of my friends declared that we couldn't be friends with the new girl in our class because she was "nothing but a redneck hillbilly." I was too worried that the group would sniff out my own hillbilly roots to say anything in the girl's defense.

Over the years, I've seen many strong mountain people take the hillbilly label and wear it proudly. As one of my friends told me, "I don't mind being called a hillbilly. Hillbilly is a culture, the culture of the mountain people. But Lord, don't call me a redneck. You can be a redneck anywhere. You can only be a hillbilly in these mountains." My opinion on the term has evolved somewhat, and sometimes I feel proud to wear the hillbilly label. But I remember what it was like, as a teenager, to lie in my bed at night and worry that I was a hillbilly; to worry that hillbilly was all the world would see when they looked at me.

While Granny was getting her treatments, Aunt Ruth was dealing with breast cancer. She'd been diagnosed for the first time shortly after marrying Sonny. I don't remember much about her reaction, probably because she kept whatever reaction she had very private. She didn't believe that wallowing in emotion made things better. I'm sure she put on a stoic face.

After two surgeries and a round of radiation therapy, the doctor announced that

Ruth's breast cancer was in remission. I stayed with her for a few days after one of her surgeries. Not because she needed the help — it never crossed my mind that I had the capacity to help Aunt Ruth — but because I was worried about her. I wanted to see her and make sure she was okay.

She was changing her dressings when I arrived, removing the bandages that covered her incisions. When she saw me standing in the hallway, she asked me to help her. I remember Ruth's no-nonsense tone about the whole thing. She wasn't embarrassed to show me her scars, the changes to her body. She told me how to remove the bandages in a matter-of-fact way, like a teacher walking a student through a math problem. Afterward, we went and made a banana pudding for a picnic the next day. It was as if nothing unusual had happened.

Now, a few years later, Aunt Ruth's breast cancer was back, on the other side. Once again, she bravely faced surgery and radiation. Even though the radiation left her bones brittle and aching, she didn't complain. I can remember her saying "Lord a night, that radiation has me feelin' like I'm on fire!" only once before she went back to her chores.

I didn't realize at the time that bilateral

breast cancer is uncommon; only a little more than 1 percent of all women with breast carcinomas have a bilateral occurrence. At the time, I thought that maybe it was just bad luck — maybe Aunt Ruth was just the one out of every hundred women who got unlucky.

Now I'm not so sure.

The health disparities in Appalachia are well documented. A comprehensive 2017 report on the state of physical and mental health in Appalachia found that this region performed worse than the national average on thirty-three out of forty-one indicators. This includes higher rates of heart disease, cancer, COPD, suicide, diabetes, injury, and stroke. It also includes more physically and mentally unhealthy days, and a greater prevalence of depression. The things that Appalachia scores better than the national average on include commute time to work, excessive drinking, and student–teacher ratio. I think most people would gladly trade the shorter commute for a lower cancer rate.

Researchers understand some of the reasons why Appalachia is less healthy than the rest of the country. For one, data shows that people from there engage in more unhealthy behaviors. Nearly one-third of Appalachians living in rural counties report being inactive, and almost a quarter are smokers. Both of these activities dramatically increase morbidity and mortality.

It's easy to blame these individuals for their poor choices. For a long time I did. I blamed Granny for starting to smoke, and other relatives for letting their weight get out of hand. I still get frustrated with one distant cousin, aged eighteen, who is so large that he struggles to sit or stand on his own. It seems so simple in abstraction: Why can't people just make healthier choices?

But I also know firsthand how hard it is to make healthy choices in Owsley County. I am a runner. I don't run fast, but most days of the week I put on my sneakers and I hit whatever road I happen to find nearby. I've found ways to run on almost every trip I've gone on: Berlin, Vietnam, New York City.

But when I am in Owsley County, I don't run. The roads are too narrow, and I'm worried about getting hit by a car on the snaking curves. I don't have cellphone service to help me navigate home if I get lost. It's unusual to see someone jogging, and I'll admit that I am self-conscious about attracting attention. I know that if I go for a run, people will talk about it. A couple of decades ago, a woman opened an aerobics studio, and the town gossip mill churned out rumors of women "hopping around in their undy-wear in front of God and everyone!" Today there are no gyms other than the one at the school.

It's also hard to find healthy food in Owsley County. The produce is limited and expensive. The best selection is at the Dollar General, which isn't exactly known for the quality of its vegetables. I am someone who eats salads on a regular basis. I have never eaten a salad in Owsley County.

I say all of this not to let people completely off the hook for their unhealthy decisions. It's not as if Appalachians are so unsophisticated and irrational that they are incapable of making good choices. People in the mountains have agency, and they use it. But environment and culture are powerful things, and they exert their influence over individuals in a complicated way. I am a person who defines myself by my healthy choices. And even I fall into a pattern of unhealthy behavior when I am in the mountains. You might as well.

But these differences in behavior don't fully account for the health disparities in Appalachia. Even when models adjust for things like the increased rates of smoking and unhealthy eating, disease rates are still higher than expected. What accounts for this difference?

The answer, I think, is environmental health hazards. There are a lot of unique and dangerous pollutants in Appalachia. Coal mining through mountaintop removal releases toxins like lead and arsenic into the streams and groundwater. The explosives used to remove parts of the mountain can launch toxic dust into the air, and this dust later settles back into the environment. Tobacco farming, too, carries health risks. Tobacco is an insect-prone crop, and those who farm it need to apply pesticides frequently and generously. Pesticides can harm farmers both through direct contact with the skin and through agrochemical contamination in the soil and water supply.

When I was a child, my mother spent a few days helping Aunt Ruth in the tobacco fields. As Wilma moved through the rows topping the tobacco, Aunt Ruth came the other way, spraying it. My mother didn't wear any protective gear that day because the family didn't own any and nobody had ever told her she needed it. She inhaled pesticides throughout the day, and, a few days later, she developed raised knots all over her legs. She went to the doctor, but he couldn't figure out what had caused the reaction. She was eventually diagnosed with a condition that roughly translates to "large red knots." The knots remained for several weeks before suddenly disappearing.

I'm not sure exactly what contaminated our well water when I was a child at Cow Creek. It could've been pesticides from the nearby tobacco fields, or an unknown contaminant from a nearby farm. All I know is that every so often the well water would get cloudy and smell funny. Granny would dump a gallon of bleach into the well, tilting the blue-and-white bottle until it was empty. We would wait a day or so to drink the water, allowing the bleach plenty of time to clear out whatever was infecting the well. If the water was clear the next day, we would resume drinking it.

Even today, many in Appalachia still struggle to access clean water. Some rural homes rely on well water because other water systems are either unavailable or unreliable. There are no federal regulations that apply to these private wells, so testing for contaminants falls on the individual property owners — many of whom don't know how to test or what to test for. Even if they did test for contaminants, their options for alternative sources of water are limited.

Those who do have access to water systems face other challenges. Martin County, Kentucky, made national headlines in 2018 when residents started posting photographs of the brown water that came out of their aging pipes. Sometimes the water tasted like Gatorade. Other times it smelled like diesel fuel. The water quality there has been poor for years; one seventeen-year-old girl has never picked up a glass, filled it with water from the tap, and drunk it. Many residents remain convinced that the town's increased cancer rates are related to contaminants in the water.

I recently had dinner with a young woman who had to cancel her trip to see her father on Christmas because of problems with the water system. "Prolly best y'all don't come down," her father said. "The water's been out for a few days and I'm not sure we'll have enough for all y'all to shower and flush the toilets." She told me that trips back to Martin County were never a sure thing given the unpredictability of the water.

Although the county is working to fix the problems with the aging water system, it's hard to find the money for a massive overhaul. The same is true across many small towns dotting the mountains. Homes are spread out, and infrastructure to connect them is expensive. Many areas don't have the resources to repair decaying roads and aging pipes. Across Central Appalachia, people collect rainwater or fill up jugs at natural springs to make sure they have the water they need.

In a world with limited resources, it can be hard to muster the political will to use tax dollars from other parts of the state or nation to fix the infrastructure in a county far away. These infrastructure problems aren't confined just to Appalachia; the water crisis in Flint, Michigan, proves that communities across America face similar challenges.

I'm sure everyone in my family has been exposed to environmental toxins over the years, be it from contaminated water, pesticides, or other unknown hazards. That's pretty much par for the course growing up in Owsley County. I'm less sure how this exposure affected us — the ways in which it harmed and changed our bodies. I worry about what I was exposed to as a child, and how it might affect my health down the road. I believe that Aunt Ruth's bilateral breast cancer was somehow tied to the environment she grew up in. I believe the same is true for the rare autoimmune condition my mother developed later in life.

There is something about the hills of Appalachia that makes the communities nestled in the hollows of them feel safe, protected, discrete. But sometimes I look at the mountains and am reminded that there are drawbacks to their power. As much as they can protect, they can also trap. They can make it harder for change, new infrastructure, new ways of life to get in. The beautiful mountains can, sometimes, be just one more barrier for people in these hills.

CHAPTER 7

It was 12:06 P.M., three minutes past when the mailman usually arrived. Over the past couple of weeks I had become an expert at tracking the movements of the mail throughout our neighborhood. Based on my calculations, the truck should be rounding the bend to our house at any second.

I went back to typing on my borrowed laptop to distract myself. I was a junior in high school, and I was taking two classes at Berea College that semester. The college had loaned me a laptop, as they did all students. It was one of the many ways Berea College worked to combat the structural disadvantages students from low-income backgrounds faced. I was grateful that I didn't have to go to a computer lab to do my homework.

It hadn't been easy to get permission to take two college classes that semester. I had thought it would be simple, since the college itself had no problem with it — I had taken a class there the previous semester and done well. It was a language class, and my mother had gotten up at six every morning to quiz me with vocabulary flash cards. I earned the top grade.

Instead, my high school took issue with the situation. "We don't want our high school girls up there with those college boys all the time," the school principal told my mother when she asked why the school had denied my request. My mother pointed out that the semester before, the school had granted two boys permission to do the same thing. The high school remained firm in its position: Girls should not spend that much time around college men. The situation — it was unclear *who* in the situation — couldn't be trusted. Plus, it just didn't look right.

My mother was irate. Her temper flared and her eyes widened. "I'm going to give you fifteen seconds to come up with another reason" — she stood up and looked down at the principal — "before I call a lawyer and a newspaper and tell them what you just said." Faced with the fury of this very short, very angry woman, the principal quickly changed his mind. My mother let him know that she was satisfied with their agreement but that she would not hesitate to visit him again if she needed to.

It seemed like there was always some sort of battle going on between my mother and the high school: the school nominated a teacher's niece for a scholarship to a summer camp even though other students were more qualified; the school wouldn't let me take the advanced math class I wanted because that "just wasn't how things were done"; a teacher sent me to the principal's office for being assertive in class while equally assertive boys faced no consequences. My mother jokes that the principal would hide in his office when he saw her coming. I think there is more than a kernel of truth in that.

My mother knew how to fight for educational opportunities, and she had learned that from Granny. When Wilma was in high school, one of the teachers started flirting with her. His advances made my mother uncomfortable, and Granny filed a complaint with the school board. Never one to sit quietly by and wait for things to happen, she also rallied other students and families behind her daughter's cause. She let it be known that this teacher was behaving inappropriately, and that he simply had to go. The school scheduled a hearing to determine whether to fire the teacher. Everyone in town was buzzing with the gossip.

During the week leading up to the school board hearing, Granny was at a laundromat in town. It was too cold to do her laundry in her yard with a hand washer as she usually did, and she was eager to finish her chores and get back home. Granny saw the teacher walking down the street, and tried to ignore him as he passed the large window at the front of the store. But the teacher gave Granny a smug smile and a suggestive wink as he walked past.

Granny leaped up with surprising speed and ran out of the laundromat. She didn't know what she was going to do with the teacher when she caught him, but she knew that she was going to hunt him down. As she ran, she grabbed a large pipe that was lying nearby. With a loud yell, she chased him through the streets of Booneville. She didn't stop until she was satisfied that she had, indeed, run him out of town. People in town laughed for weeks about the terrified look on his face as he fled the crazed woman wielding a rusty pipe. "I believe she meaned to kill him," Aunt Ruth said.

The school board eventually voted to fire the teacher. In some places that might have been seen as punishment enough. Not so in the hills of Eastern Kentucky. This wasn't the first time the teacher had flirted with a young student, and in the mountains, anyone who hurts a child is a fair target for vigilante justice.

Granny once told me about a man accused of molesting a child. A jury acquitted him on a technicality, but the entire town remained convinced of his guilt. Shortly after he left the courthouse, reveling in his freedom, another man shot him dead. The shooter didn't know the accused man; he had never met him before in his life. But, he said, "someone had to get justice for those chil'ren." The shooter drove to the sheriff's office afterward and turned himself in.

The fate of the teacher was not quite so harsh, but the community punished him nevertheless. The next semester the teacher approached a group of high school students on a school bus and tried to make conversation with them. He figured the whole incident had blown over, and he was ready to rebuild his reputation. Getting back into the good graces of the students seemed like the place to start.

The students were having no such thing. At first they ignored the teacher as he stood beside the school bus and spoke to them through the windows. But they soon realized that the teacher wasn't going away, and, even more irritating, he was starting to whine about them ignoring him.

It started off with one male student unzipping his pants. A few others quickly joined in. It took the teacher a few moments to realize what was happening. By the time he figured out that the students were peeing on him, he was already damp. When the teacher tried to file a complaint against the boys with the principal, the principal said, "I don't know what you're talking about. Those boys would never do that. Don't be lyin' on those young uns," and he sent the teacher away.

I loved the college classes I took at Berea. They were challenging, forcing me to think about different things in different ways. I took a job at a small used-book store near campus, and I chatted with the students who would drop by in between classes. In between customers, I read books about philosophy, art, and politics. The owner of the bookstore, a retired professor, talked to me about things like the size of the universe and the relativity of time.

Berea High School seemed lackluster in comparison. There were some outstanding teachers — like Ms. Carpenter, the science instructor who stayed late a day each week to let me spend extra time in the lab, and Ms. Moran, who nurtured my love of writing. But some of the teachers had little interest in actually teaching students. One instructor spent class time telling students how to make pot brownies. Another turned on the television every day and said that watching the news was "education enough." Still another spent the first few minutes of class trading makeup tips with her favorite students. It wasn't surprising to me that the high school performed poorly on state-level assessments.

Berea High School was small, the kind of small where everyone knows everything you do. I once skipped the period after lunch to hang out with my friends at the Burger King in town. My mom knew about it before I got home that evening. And, while there was comfort in being friends with the same group of girls I had been friends with since first grade, I was tired of retelling the same stories we had told for a decade. There was a set order to our lives and our relationships with one another.

I always tried to look like someone who had it all together. I played several sports, got good grades, and had enough friends.

But as I entered high school, my carefully constructed façade began to crack under the small-town pressure. In hindsight it all seems petty: My boyfriend broke up with me and began to date my best friend. I signed up for too many activities and was only mediocre at all of them. All of my friends were in the homecoming court except me. One of my dance instructors poked my stomach and noted that I was "getting a little soft." For someone who tried to convince the world that she was perfect, who expected herself to be perfect, it suddenly seemed like a lot to bear.

I wonder if my need for perfection came from my mother. From watching her obsess over her grades and performance. From seeing her work late into the night preparing three types of dessert for Christmas when one dessert would have done. From the way everything she did was just a little more elaborate than it needed to be. In some ways I am grateful that I inherited this drive; it propelled me toward success. But it took me years to rein it in — to understand that it would never be satisfied.

Faced with the feeling that my perfect world, my perfect self, was falling apart, I started to think about ways to get out of Berea. I wanted to go somewhere new, where nobody knew my teenage failures and high school humiliations. My parents had made it clear from the time I was young that I was going to college, and I figured that would be a good opportunity to start afresh.

The school was little help. There was a guidance counselor who was supposed to assist us with college selection starting our junior year, but I remember only one meeting with her. I showed her a list of colleges I wanted to go to, including Yale, Harvard, and Wellesley. She sort of giggled when she looked at the list and said, "Well, whatever. You have a good GPA. Give it a shot." She didn't elaborate much on what "giving it a shot" entailed, or what steps I needed to take to apply. She left it to me to figure out these application processes. I'm sure she assumed that I'd get in to some school somewhere. Maybe not the Ivy League, but, after all, what kid from Berea had ever gotten in to an Ivy?

I remember the day the brochure for the United World College arrived in my mailbox. Instead of a college, this brochure was for a high school. And not just a high school, but a boarding school, set far away in the mountains of New Mexico, that lasted for the senior year of high school and one additional year. I had never been to New Mexico, and I was fascinated by the image of the mountains rising up out of the desert.

UWC had around two hundred students, representing approximately eighty different countries. The school's mission was to explore and celebrate diversity — it believed that you create world peace by building connections between people from different parts of the globe. Each student had a roommate from a different continent. The school's curriculum was based around understanding the diversity of the students on campus.

Even better, the school was free for every American student it accepted. I had already started worrying about the cost of college, wondering how I was going to be able to afford the $40,000-plus-a-year price tag at many of the schools I was interested in. This free education seemed too good to be true. Things seemed even better when I learned that graduates of UWC automatically qualified for significant scholarships to pay for college.

As soon as I read the brochure, I decided to apply.

At first, my mother wasn't a fan of the idea. She kept saying "We'll see" and changing the subject each time I brought it up. She had just left her job in insurance sales — as good as she was at it, she didn't really enjoy it and the hours were long. "I wouldn't change places with you for the world," Ruth told her, "havin' to work all of those hours. Your job will always be there, Wilma; your family won't." Plus, Granny was getting sicker, and my mother was increasingly in charge of caring for her. And, as I felt my constructed exterior shatter, I was beginning to rebel — staying out too late and hanging around people I knew I shouldn't be with. My mother decided that it made sense for her to spend a few months at home. She wasn't ready for me to leave the house as soon as she began to spend more time in it.

Still, my mother never told me not to apply. I give her — and my equally supportive father — a lot of credit for this. She had never told me not to do anything. Anytime I wanted to take on an activity, she was encouraging. When I asked her to drive me to audition for a community theater production, she didn't once point out that I had no experience acting or singing. She wasn't about to start restricting what I thought I could do. Aunt Ruth was also supportive. "That sounds like a real adventure!" she told me. "It's sure a long way from home, but you'll be all right."

Granny, on the other hand, was worried. She had never traveled much. I'm pretty sure the only time she left Kentucky was a few years after Papaw died, when she decided she wanted to see the beach at least once and went to Virginia with a friend. Although Granny was proud of me for wanting to get an education, she didn't understand why I had to travel quite so far from home to do it. It didn't help that her geography was a bit confused. No matter how many times I explained to her that I was going to school in *New* Mexico, she kept asking me about my application to the school in Mexico. She seemed concerned that I wouldn't be able to communicate with anyone there since I didn't speak Spanish.

In my conversations with her, I heard echoes of Papaw's pleas to Wilma years before. "Please, child, don't leave your home. Don't leave your family. This is where you belong." I could feel the same tug-of-war that my mother must've felt: the weight of the mountains anchoring me where I stood. I wanted desperately to break free, to shatter that sense of familiarity that was holding me back. At the same time, the mountains were my foundation, my context. I wasn't sure who I would be outside of them.

The week that UWC released its decisions, I went home each day to wait for the mailman. He tended to come during my lunchtime, and as soon as the lunch bell rang I dashed out to my car and drove the couple of miles home. If he hadn't shown up by the time I arrived, Granny, my mother, and I drove around the neighborhood just to see if we could spot the mail truck. As soon as it arrived, I rushed out to the mailbox to check if there was a letter with the UWC logo.

The letter finally came. It was in a thin envelope, but I was too naïve about admissions processes to know that a thin envelope usually means bad news. I ran into the house and walked to the corner where I had been typing on my laptop just a few minutes before. I felt a surge of adrenaline as I tore the letter open. I felt nauseous after reading the first paragraph.

"I got in," I turned and told my mother. She and Granny erupted into happy hoots and hollers. "Wee boy!" Granny shouted, clapping her hands. They both had their concerns about this new life path I was choosing, but they weren't going to let their concerns spoil a perfectly fine celebration. Later that evening we sat on the front porch talking about all of the possibilities that lay before me.

There was never any question that I would go. Two free years at an incredible, unique boarding school? College scholarships after that? You couldn't turn down that kind of opportunity. *I* couldn't turn down that kind of opportunity.

Still, as the summer began, my last summer at home, I almost wished I had never seen that brightly colored United World College brochure. I hadn't realized how much home mattered to me until I was faced with leaving it. New Mexico suddenly felt very far away. I knew there were mountains there. But I also knew they wouldn't be my mountains.

■ ■ ■ ■ ■

PART II
AWAY

■ ■ ■ ■ ■

PART II
AWAY

CHAPTER 8

UWC was different than I expected. I had been outside of the United States only once, when my parents and I visited my father's sister in California and walked across the United States–Mexico border to spend a few hours in Tijuana. I expected everyone at UWC to show up in strange-looking clothes and listen to strange-sounding music. I pictured boys in flowing robes and girls in elaborate headpieces. Most kids showed up in jeans and listened to American pop music.

A girl from Pakistan met our car when we pulled up to campus. We parked and followed her into the dorm. "This way," she said as she beckoned us. She pointed out important landmarks as she went. "This is where your residential adviser lives. Those are condoms on the door. People do have sex here." My somewhat conservative parents looked alarmed. I think, in that moment, they considered loading me into the car and taking me back to Kentucky.

Instead, they unloaded the fully packed minivan we had driven more than twenty hours from Kentucky. My mother was worried about leaving me so far from home, and to ease her own mind, she had hauled everything I could possibly need across the country. She brought me two umbrellas, even though I reminded her several times that I was moving to a desert.

That first night in the dorm I cried. My roommate, a quiet girl from Eastern Europe, had gone to bed early. She was jetlagged, and we had struggled to make conversation. Her English was stilted, and I didn't know what questions to ask her. I had never heard of her country until a few hours before. I didn't want to show my ignorance. I think she was irritated that she had an American roommate. The American government was unpopular at UWC because of its involvement in the Middle East. Plus, my classmates told me time and again, "Americans have no culture." That was news to me.

The first few days on campus were a blur of new people. I couldn't pronounce many of my classmates' names, so I avoided directly addressing people. Instead I would look right at them and speak a little too loudly, hoping to attract their attention.

It was the first time I'd been around so much diversity. Owsley County is more than 98 percent white, 0.5 percent black, and 1.4 percent Latinx. Madison County, where Berea is located, is almost as homogeneous, at nearly 92 percent white. Most people I knew growing up were white and identified as Christian. I didn't have a lot of experience with people who didn't look like me.

My parents had always taught me to value diversity — including racial diversity. My mom bought me both black and white dolls when I was a child, and we were a host family for an international college student from Nepal for a couple of years. But most of what I knew about race was abstract, about the *idea* of respecting differences rather than how to actually do it.

I don't often talk about how racially homogeneous the places I spent my childhood are because I think it perpetuates an inaccurate stereotype about Appalachia: the idea that it's full of nothing but white people. I know that's not true. There are people of color in the mountains too. In Lynch, a small former coal outpost, the majority of the town's residents are black. Black coal miners have historically made up between 20 and 50 percent of the workforce in some parts of this region. Frank X Walker, a black writer from rural Kentucky, started the Affrilachian Poets to showcase diverse artistic voices in the mountains. My childhood in Appalachia didn't include many experiences with racial diversity, and I was worse off for it. But not all places in Appalachia suffer from that deficit.

In those first days at UWC, I was becoming aware of how ignorant I was about the larger world. A few weeks after I arrived, a boy in the neighboring dorm asked, in front of a group, if I could point to Iraq on a map. "Of course I can," I lied. He went to his room to get a map to make me prove it, and I found an excuse to scamper away. The next week, I went to a girl from an East Asian country to ask for help with my math homework. She informed me, with an annoyed look on her face, that she was "more of an arts type" before unceremoniously ushering me out of her room.

We were all feeling out of place at the beginning. My roommate cried one night because she was tired of having to speak English all the time. One of my Scandinavian friends called home three times in one day to ask his dad to send him his favorite foods. A student in a neighboring dorm blasted African music at all hours because he wanted to be surrounded by the sounds of his home.

Over time, we formed relationships to create an ad hoc family. We had state-mates (who were from the same state), country-mates (who were from the same country), wall-mates (who shared a wall in the dorms), language-mates (who shared the same language), and on and on. We were all far from home. We formed community however and wherever we could.

Once a month, we had "community meetings," where the administration, the staff, and the entire student body came together to discuss the issues that were affecting the school. When we talked of our concerns about our community, you could see differences in how we thought, how we made decisions, what we valued. At one meeting, someone from the administration gave us a lecture about drinking on campus. Many of the European students were old enough to buy alcohol in their home countries, and they would sometimes sneak a bottle of vodka or gin into their suitcases to bring back to campus after the holidays. At the end of the administration's lecture, the two French students on campus stood up. "This is so stupid!" they exclaimed. "Why can we not have a glass of wine in the evenings?" They proceeded to argue at length in support of not just allowing students to drink on campus, but also of providing them with an on-campus pub to do so. No matter how many times the administration explained that American law simply would not allow it, the French students remained unconvinced. At one point, one of them stormed outside to have a cigarette.

I missed my family and friends terribly. Almost everything reminded me of them. The smell of cookies baking in the dining hall made me think of my mother; meeting a student with the same name as my best friend made me catch my breath. We weren't allowed to have cellphones on campus, so I would wait in line in the evenings to use the one phone in my dorm. It was in a closet with a clear door that people could see through, and I tried to keep my emotions in check when other people were nearby. My mother mailed me what seemed like a lifetime supply of calling cards. One time when I called home, she told me that she couldn't talk; she had invited several of my friends over for homemade pizza, and it was time to eat. I wondered if it was too late to go back to Berea. I understood why my mother had cried every night of her first semester at college.

There weren't many students like me on campus. There were about twenty Americans in my year, but most of them came from other parts of the country. Many of them had dual citizenships and had lived or traveled abroad. There was one girl from West Virginia in the year above me, but she was quiet and studied a lot. She told me she was going to go back to West Virginia for college the next year because she missed home. I think the fact that she was homesick herself made her less able to see my loneliness.

Back then, most of my wardrobe consisted of faded bell-bottom jeans and bright T-shirts. I wore thick liquid eyeliner and blow-dried my hair to give it volume. I felt garish and showy sometimes compared to my international classmates, who wore stylish scarves and minimal makeup. It had never occurred to me that scarves served any purpose other than keeping your neck warm in the wintertime. Part of me wanted to dress more like them, but part of me wasn't sure how to. I felt a tension about the whole thing: On the one hand I was striving to be as Kentucky as I could because we were supposed to represent our cultures; on the other I was trying to tone down my Kentuckiness to fit in to this new environment.

It was also difficult adjusting to the rigorous academic standards. Since many U.S. colleges do not offer financial aid for international students, the UWC's promise of college scholarships was the best shot some of my classmates had to afford an American college education. This led to a fierce competition for slots in many countries. Some African countries selected students based solely on their performance on national-level tests, and my classmates had received the single highest scores on their country's examinations. Other places selected students based on their family's position in the government. The prince of Greece had graduated from UWC the year before I arrived there. The princess of Belgium enrolled in 2018.

On my first day of science class, the teacher began the lesson by saying, "So we all remember this from our previous schooling, yes?" He quickly scrawled some scientific terms on the board. Everyone else nodded and looked bored, so I did too. But I wrote in my notes, *Figure out what mitosis is.*

My classmates seemed to know more than me, to be better prepared than me. This was especially embarrassing because I, unlike the vast majority of my peers, was attending school in my home country. We were being taught in my native language. I felt that somehow this should give me an advantage. I was ashamed of my mediocre grades my first semester.

Eventually, though, I settled in. I made friends with a boy from Norway, a girl from Massachusetts, a boy from Venezuela. I learned to play Oasis songs on my guitar, and we stayed up after curfew singing in my dorm room. I had never had to make new friends before, and I was relieved to find that I could do it. The girl from West Virginia and I organized a Southern dinner and made fried chicken. There weren't a lot of students from the South, so we got creative with the guest list. The European kid whose dad had worked in Alabama for a year got an invitation. So did the boy who grew up in the Virginia part of the Washington, D.C., suburbs.

I joined the wilderness training program on campus, which trained students to lead backcountry trips in the New Mexico mountains. I wasn't great at the whole wilderness thing. I accidentally set the campus lawn on fire when we were learning to use the cookstoves. I got lost for an hour during the map navigation class and waited on a rock for someone to find me. I sat down in a snowbank during the one and only winter camping trip I went on. A girl from Lebanon and I decided we were so cold and miserable that we just couldn't snowshoe any farther. Our Dutch friend snorted at us and pulled us to our feet. "Warm-weather people," he muttered to himself, half amused, half irritated.

But, as much as I hated the logistics of backpacking, I felt at home in the mountains. Although the scenery looked a bit different, the hills still rolled into the distance in familiar waves. The earth smelled the same after it rained. Bird songs sounded the same when they echoed off the mountains.

Sometimes, when I was particularly homesick, I would hike up the hill behind campus and look out at the desert below. If I turned and looked one way, all I could see was flat and sand. If I turned and looked the other, all I could see was cascading hills. When I was seated where the mountains met the desert, this place didn't feel that different from Berea, where the Appalachians met the flatland.

Over time, I got better at studying. Part of it was just realizing that I did, in fact, have to study — I had never had to study for high school classes before. I found a comfortable chair in the library and set up shop. I would often work until curfew, scurry back to my room for bed checks, then keep working until the wee hours of the morning. I pulled my first all-nighter, using instant coffee and the homemade brownies my mother had sent me to stay awake. My grades, and my waistline, increased my second semester.

By the end of my first year on campus I was sad to leave the diverse little bubble we had created. Although I was returning the next year, the second-year students were not. I knew that they would scatter, going off to colleges and universities around the world. I also knew that I would never see most of them again. My world was becoming larger, more fluid, more filled with change.

The summer after my first year at UWC, I spent a lot of time with Granny in Owsley County. She was increasingly frail, and my mother and I went down to see her as often as we could. She stayed with us some as well, but she insisted more and more that she wanted to be at home: in her space, with her friends, her community, and her belongings. She still hid ice cream for me in her freezer and sneaked me money to buy things I needed for school. She listened to me play guitar and tapped her foot along to the music. She asked me if there were any cute boys in Mexico, then asked to see pictures when I told her there were. She didn't understand how we could communicate since I still didn't speak Spanish very well. Aunt Ruth was around that summer too, asking lots of questions about my new life and if I liked it. "I'd like to try me some of that," she said, after I told her about a place in town with really good salsa verde.

We talked a lot about college that summer, my parents, Granny, and I. UWC had an excellent college-admissions counselor. He had insisted that we make a list of schools we planned to apply to before we went home for the summer. He talked us through specific strategies and requirements for each place on our lists. I spent the summer obsessing over admissions rates and average SAT scores.

Most of the schools I was looking at were places Granny had never heard of — small liberal arts colleges in states far away. Yet, despite their unfamiliarity, Granny listened to me explain the schools on the list with joy and attentiveness. "Ah, boy, that one sounds like a good one," she would say after I told her about each one.

I know she was proud of me. Proud that I

was planning on going to college. Proud that her grandchild was going so much further than she had been able to, than even my mother had been able to. I could see it in her eyes each time we talked about colleges. I think I also saw a bit of wistfulness.

It was hard to say goodbye to Granny at the end of the summer. I hadn't said it out loud — none of us had — but I knew she wasn't going to live much longer. Then again, it didn't seem possible that Granny could die. She had been very sick for many years, and in some ways it seemed like death had decided it didn't want to mess with this feisty little mountain woman.

The day I returned to UWC, I used an old boom box to record myself playing and singing Granny's favorite song. It was written by Pat Humphries and called "Swimming to the Other Side." The chorus proclaimed:

We are living 'neath the great big dipper,
We are washed by the very same rain,
We are swimming in this stream together,
Some in power and some in pain,
We can worship this ground we walk on,
Cherishing the beings that we live beside,
Loving spirits will live forever,
We're all swimming to the other side.

"Ain't that something?" Granny would say each time I played it. "I sure do love that song."

I got back to campus a week early for wilderness training. I was a team leader that year, which meant that I would lead a group of first-year students on a three-day orientation trip into the New Mexico mountains. We had a refresher trip the week before they arrived, to brush up on our skills and reduce the likelihood of losing or maiming the incoming students. My co-leader reminded me to rehydrate the lentils properly this time, so as to avoid a repeat of the stomach issues my cooking had caused everyone on our last trip.

I remember the sense of freedom I felt on that excursion. The New Mexico mountains felt welcoming. It felt good to reconnect with friends. We sat around in a circle as the sun set and talked about our summers and our plans for the year. That night I slept outside, under the stars, and marveled at the vastness of everything.

I knew something was wrong as soon as we arrived back on campus. A friend, who had been watching for our bus to arrive, pulled me aside as soon as we unloaded. "You need to go call your family," he said. I didn't go to the phone booth straightaway. I unloaded the backpacking gear and took a shower. I didn't want to hear the news I knew was coming: Granny had died. She had swum to the other side.

Granny's funeral was filled with music: bright, fast, mountain tunes that rang out of the chapel and echoed off the mountains. I noticed some people's feet tapping as the musicians played and sang. I knew she would have been pleased. We buried her next to Papaw, on the top of a hill that looked over a beautiful holler.

After Granny's funeral, my mother told me what joy Granny had gotten from the tape I'd made for her before I went back to school. She listened to it daily, my mother said. One time, Granny's breathing grew labored and she was in and out of consciousness. Her children gathered around her bed to say their goodbyes. My mother put on the tape so that I, far away on a mountain in New Mexico, could say goodbye in my own way. A few measures into the song, Granny arose from her apparent coma and began clapping her hands. "What's everyone lookin' so sad for?" she said as she began singing along. Everyone laughed.

I know Granny is still singing and laughing in the mountains somewhere. Sometimes she sends us small signs. A few months after Granny's death, my mother visited her grave. Overwhelmed with how much she missed Granny, my mother began to weep. Out of nowhere, a bird came diving down from the sky. Granny had always loved birds — she kept a pair of "love birds" in her trailer and put hummingbird feeders in her yard. When the bird flew in between my mother's legs, she cried out and ran a few feet away from the grave. The bird followed. It continued to flit and flap around my mother's head until both she and my father burst into laughter.

Later that fall, I received my college acceptance letter. I had applied early decision to Wellesley College, an all-women's school near Boston. I had known about Wellesley before I went to UWC — it was always near the top in the list of colleges that I pored over. But I think, in part, I had chosen Wellesley because a lot of my friends were applying there. The school had a strong relationship with UWC, so it felt like somewhere safe and known.

But I also applied to Wellesley because I was afraid to apply anywhere else. I was still struggling with a need to be perfect, or at least to seem perfect. And that was hard to do when I compared myself to my UWC classmates. They spoke multiple languages, won national awards for mathematics, traveled to multiple continents. They were the ones who should go to Harvard, Yale, Princeton. I was not. I didn't want to embarrass myself by trying, and inevitably failing, to compete with them. Despite being an excellent school, Wellesley had a higher acceptance rate than many schools of equal caliber, probably because of its naturally smaller applicant pool. It seemed like a good compromise: I could go to an incredibly well-respected school without risking failure.

It was uncomfortable to look back on how far I had come from where I'd started. I felt lucky to be where I was. And I don't mean lucky in the sense that I was merely appreciative of the opportunities before me. I knew — I still know — that there were many students in both Berea and Owsley County who were just as smart as me. My friend Matthew had regularly scored higher than me on tests. My friend Anne Marie outdid me in most subjects as well. My cousin Melissa was just as bright as me when we were children.

I now had advantages that these friends

and family members did not. I had a supportive school with a talented college-
admissions counselor who had connections
to the best universities in the country. Many
of my Berea classmates had received little
guidance in the application process. Some
of them had decided not to bother applying
at all, and made choices that would alter
their lives forever. Melissa had dropped out
of high school and eloped with her boyfriend
on her eighteenth birthday. A few months
later she announced she was pregnant.
When Aunt Ruth begged her to finish high
school, she said, "Why, Lord-a-mercy no!
I'm a married woman now."

In light of all of this, I felt that my opportunities were precarious, that I was one
bad step away from being right back where
I'd started. It's not that it was a bad place
to be, Berea. It's just that I — more so with
each day — defined myself as someone who
achieved. And for many years, I would
believe that achieving meant staying outside
of the community that had formed me.

The post office was located at the bottom
of the hill that UWC sat on. I opened my
Wellesley acceptance letter as soon as I
pulled it from the mailbox. I didn't feel
excited. Instead, I breathed a sigh of relief.
I was going to college, to a good college. As

I walked back up the hill toward campus, I thought about all of the ways I was headed up.

CHAPTER 9

Wellesley College looks like a postcard. Trees line the perimeter of the campus, making it feel separate, distinct from the surrounding community — a world unto itself. The brick and stone buildings possess a sort of European charm. There are hidden passages and unexpected balconies.

During the first-year activities fair, I signed up for something approaching twenty different clubs. If I wasn't sure what a club was, I still put my name down just in case I might be interested. I ran for class vice president, though no one knew me and I didn't realize I needed to campaign. I lost the race handily.

Electoral defeats aside, I still thought I had an advantage in this new environment: I had lived away from home for two years, and the extra year in New Mexico meant I was older than most entering students. Plus, I had ten or so UWC classmates joining me on campus. Even my roommate, a friendly Latvian who borrowed my socks without asking, was a UWC alumna. I set big goals for myself: I was going to do it all. Study hard, be social, be involved in my community.

This felt achievable at Wellesley. People were welcoming, and it didn't take much effort to get involved. I ended up joining far too many of those clubs I'd signed up for, including a modern dance class. I was the worst student in the group by far — I fell down at least twice per class — but everyone was supportive. "You did so much better today," one upperclasswoman told me on a regular basis. It was code for "You weren't as terribly-awfully-horrible today as you were last week," but it always made me smile. Wellesley is a school founded on and designed around female empowerment. Most of the women I met took this value to heart.

I had always been quiet in my classes at UWC. I was never confident that I had the right answer. Even if we were just telling anecdotes about our different cultural experiences, I was always sure someone had an experience more interesting than mine. After the 2004 election, UWC students were discussing the presidential outcome. I listened to their theories about why Americans had voted for George W. Bush over John Kerry, but I didn't weigh in. Even though I was the only American in that room, I still felt that their opinions were more valid than mine.

At Wellesley, I learned to speak up. The school was always talking about how this was a place for women to find their voices. I took that literally. It wasn't comfortable to express an opinion in front of a hundred-person lecture hall — my hands would shake and my voice would crack — but it got slightly less terrifying each time I did it. At least twice I had older students come up to me after a class and tell me, "I really enjoyed what you had to say."

Of course there were pockets of exclusivity set apart from this backdrop of inclusion. In the spring of my first year, I tried to join one of the societies on campus. Ostensibly, these societies were founded to promote different causes: the arts, classics, politics. Yet many of them functioned like sororities, full of women from elite New England prep schools and California private academies. I think I wanted to join a society because it felt like they offered a piece of the college experience I was missing. They had parties. Sometimes they had parties with men. It all sounded very exciting. Plus, I wanted to prove to myself that I could belong there, with these women who seemed so sophisticated and worldly.

Each of the societies hosted a series of teas as part of the selection process, basically "meet and greets" where the current members got to size up the prospective applicants. I showed up at my first tea in tight-fitting jeans with rhinestones and a baggy sweater. I immediately felt out of place. My jeans were a few shades too light, and my shirt was made out of the wrong material. I didn't have a headband or pearl earrings. My hair wasn't straight enough or shiny enough. I was disappointed when I didn't get in, but not terribly surprised.

Thankfully, I had my fellow UWC grads to keep my spirits up. There were enough of us on campus that we remained an ad hoc family. We made cakes for one another's birthdays and studied together at the Starbucks in town. We played the songs that had been popular at UWC, and looked through old photographs of ourselves in New Mexico. We stayed up too late and had one too many glasses of wine.

I didn't know any Wellesley students from Kentucky. I don't think I knew any from Appalachia. I'm sure they were there, these other mountain transplants. But I didn't miss their presence in the same way I had at UWC. I had learned to create other identities and communities. At that point, my roots in Eastern Kentucky were no longer the only thing grounding me.

My first experience with the Ivy League came on a Friday night. There was a bus that would take women from Wellesley into Boston, and one of its stops was in Harvard Square. A few of my UWC classmates were attending Harvard, and we thought it would be fun to have a spontaneous reunion. We met at a restaurant to catch up on gossip about our new lives and former classmates.

After dinner, one of my UWC classmates, a year ahead of me, invited us to come and hang out at his finals club. I didn't know what a finals club was, but I soon discovered that Harvard has all-male exclusive social clubs — like fraternities but with a more monied, privileged ambience. We walked the few short blocks to the club and went in the basement entrance.

There were a lot of men and a few women hanging out in the largely windowless room. My friends went to grab drinks, and I somehow found myself surrounded by unfamiliar Harvard men. "Wow, this is a nice place," I told one of them. It wasn't really — it looked like your typical college living room with an added sense of faded grandeur — but I was trying to make small talk. "What's the rest of it like?" It was clear that we were in a very small part of a much larger house.

"Like something you're not going to see," he responded. "Only members get to go upstairs. And certainly not women." He looked at me as though he expected me to be impressed. I wasn't sure how to react, so I quickly found a reason to leave the conversation.

I went to parties at finals clubs several more times after that. In many ways, I hated the institutions. The way the all-male membership got to control access to these places of perceived power. The way the men selected the women to allow in at the door as though they were selecting sandwiches at a deli counter. The way some men would turn up their noses at me whenever I told them I went to Wellesley. "Are you planning to get your MRS degree?" one asked, bursting into laughter at his joke about marriage. In general, the men seemed to assume that I, and every other Wellesley woman, would fall all over them. They had, in their view, deigned to let us into their exclusive clubs.

There was a pervasive sense that we should be grateful.

And — as much as I hate to admit it — there were times when I *did* feel grateful. I felt like I had accomplished something when I was invited — I made sure to tell women from the societies that had rejected me that I had spent the previous evening at a finals club. At those parties, I was passing for privileged in one of the most privileged environments in the world. It turns out that my college-self was willing to put up with a decent amount of chauvinism for that feeling.

Toward the end of my first year at Wellesley, I began to date a guy from an Ivy League school. His name was Diego, and he went to Princeton. He had been a year ahead of me at UWC. I hadn't known him well at school; he was part of a cooler crowd than I was. I remember watching him at UWC as he meandered around campus with his rowdy and confident group of friends. I would look the other way when I saw them coming — I felt anxious when they were around, worried that they would ignore me. Or, even worse, that they wouldn't and I'd have to figure out something cool to say.

The day Diego got in to college, he walked

into one of his final exams in swim trunks, carrying a boom box. He spent five minutes scribbling a few words on the paper, then walked out and headed to the pool. This exit, and Diego in general, became UWC legend. He was smart, handsome, and uninterested in taking orders from anyone.

Diego and I reconnected at a party hosted by some UWC classmates, just a few weeks before summer. I was going to be in D.C. that summer for an internship, and he told me his family lived nearby. He said we'd be in touch. I almost hoped we wouldn't — I still got nervous when he was around. He always looked at me with a wry smile and a slightly tilted head. I could never tell what he was thinking.

But he set out to win me over that summer. He picked me up from my internship and took me to an expensive French café to eat madeleines for lunch. He told me not to worry when lunch ran long — after all, he said, "it's just an internship." He cooked me Mediterranean food in my apartment, and we had a picnic on the roof. When I returned to college, he gave me an expensive necklace for my birthday. He told me he loved me, and that our relationship was the most important thing in the world. He struck me as very old, very wise, and very mature.

When Diego took me to New York, to a party with his Princeton friends at a fancy penthouse, he gave me instructions on how to behave. "Don't be too loud," he warned me. I heard the "they'll find you irritating" at the end of that sentence, even though he didn't say it. Once we were at the party he pointed to people in the room and recited the names of the companies where their fathers were CEOs. I didn't know most of the companies, but I raised my eyebrows and pretended to be as impressed as he wanted me to be. This was his world. I was a guest in it at his invitation. As with the finals clubs, I was happy to be allowed in.

But after a few months, I began noticing things about Diego that bothered me. If I went to Boston for a night without him, he would ask me if there'd been any men in the group I was with. If I said yes, he would interrogate me about the evening, lecture me about how it looked suspicious for me to spend time with other men. Once, a coed group of friends and I hung out in the living room of a male dorm, and Diego raged for an hour about the impropriety of it all. He threatened to break up with me because I entered a ballroom dance competition without telling him about it. Ballroom dancing was far too sexy an activity for his girlfriend to participate in.

He suddenly didn't like my friends. Although he'd been friends with some of them at the beginning, now he thought they were too promiscuous, too trashy, not a good influence. None of this was true, of course, but it was true to him. He once didn't speak to me for an entire four-hour car ride because I told his cousin, who was in the car with us, a funny story about a friend of mine kissing someone at a debate tournament. "I thought you said she was a good person!" he screamed at me when I asked him why he was ignoring me. "She's a slut and you lied to me." His cousin gave me a sympathetic look as Diego resumed his silence.

Diego found ways to make me feel inferior, and a favorite was the fact that I didn't go to an Ivy League school. He let it be known that while Wellesley was acceptable, it was nowhere near the category of Princeton. He once told me he liked that I went to a school for women who were "smart but not too smart."

Still, he was funny, confident, sometimes sweet. After we fought he would buy me presents and tell me how wonderful I was.

We went on adventures, like taking the Greyhound to D.C. for the weekend or riding the train to New York City for the evening. We once went to Newport, Rhode Island, and spent the day walking hand in hand along the beach, talking about our future together. My emotions regarding him were complicated, changing wildly on any given day.

I took Diego home to meet my family one school break. We went to Owsley County for an afternoon, because Aunt Ruth had wanted to meet "this young feller my niece has been a-courtin'." Ruth and Sonny welcomed Diego into their home the best they knew how. Ruth couldn't pronounce his name, but she apologized and, with a big smile, said, "We'll just call you Dave." She made corn bread and soup beans, and we ate in her small kitchen. I could see Diego's eyes growing wide as Ruth and Sonny ate with their hands and talked with their mouths full.

He didn't say anything then, but his feelings came out in a fight just a few months later. He was visiting me for a few days, and I had made him mad for some reason or other. Probably because I had dinner with a friend he didn't like, or didn't call him back quickly enough. The fight quickly escalated.

"You? Who are you?" he screamed at me, his eyes wide. "I'm something. I matter." He said the words he knew would hurt me: "You're nothing but a redneck from a redneck family. You don't even matter."

He stormed out of the room, and I began to sob. Somehow he had figured it out: I was afraid that I would never belong in his high-society world.

The next day I downloaded applications to transfer to Ivy League schools. Most of my decision was motivated by anger — I was angry at Diego for thinking that I didn't belong, couldn't belong, in institutions of such privilege. I was going to show him he was wrong.

But I think part of my decision was motivated by fear, insecurity. I had stood on the periphery of the Ivy League that year, and I had never felt truly welcome. Maybe Diego was right. Maybe I really didn't matter. Maybe going to one of these schools was the only thing that would make me matter. I never expected to get in, but I was glad I had finally taken my shot.

A few months later I received my acceptance letter to Yale. I remember feeling something akin to confusion when I saw the large envelope stuffed in my college mailbox. I'd almost forgotten that I'd applied.

My first emotion when I read the letter was elation. I was going to belong. In the Ivy League. My mind raced, thinking in feelings instead of words.

Then I felt uncertain. It was late spring by the time I received the acceptance letter. I had less than two months on campus before I would leave for the summer. If I was going to transfer to Yale — and I knew from the moment I opened that envelope that I would transfer to Yale — I wouldn't come back to Wellesley. I had spent a lot of time building a world for myself in this place. Even in the midst of my roller-coaster relationship with Diego, it was a place where I felt welcome. I had deep friendships and casual acquaintances. I couldn't believe that I was willingly walking away from it all.

But, at that time, I was someone who placed the possibility of achievement over existing relationships. Maybe it started when I left Berea to go to UWC — when I walked away from everything and everyone I knew in order to pursue an opportunity outside of the mountains. Maybe I believed that in order to become the person I wanted to be, I had to blindly chase objective achievements.

My mother was over the moon when I told her I was going to Yale. I remember calling her on my cellphone from the student center and hearing the awe in her voice. For the next week, she answered her phone with "Hello, this is the mother of an Ivy League student." Aunt Ruth was similarly impressed. "Well, Yale, now, that's a fancy school," she told me proudly.

The rest of my Owsley County family was less excited. I announced I was transferring to Yale at a family birthday party. "Huh," Dale said, a flicker of wariness in his eyes. He knew that he didn't understand this world I was part of, and he wasn't going to talk about something so unfamiliar to him. "I may be an old ignorant hillbilly," Dale says often, "but I know enough not to let anyone else figure it out." The rest of the family offered faint words of congratulations before moving on to talk about my cousin's new girlfriend. I wondered, in that moment, if I had my values wrong. I wondered if my mother had felt the same way when she'd told her family about her acceptance to Berea College years before.

My parents picked me up from Wellesley at the end of the year. I was perfectly capable of driving myself home to Kentucky, but they wanted to see Yale, and this gave them the perfect opportunity. We drove back to Kentucky through Connecticut and stopped in New Haven. I felt a small prick of pride when I stepped onto campus for the first time. I made sure to tell anyone at the tour who would listen, "I'll be going here this fall." There was something freeing about being an admitted student there. I still wasn't sure I belonged, but I knew I could at least fake it well enough for others to believe that I did.

Diego had told me he was proud of me for getting in to Yale, but I don't think he liked it, deep down. I think it threatened him that I was on equal footing with him, made him feel as though he had less power in the relationship.

Not too long after I arrived at Yale, he screamed at me during yet another fight, "Do you want me to break up with you? Is that it?"

"No," I responded calmly. "I'm breaking up with you." I hung up the phone, waiting for the emotions to hit me. I expected to feel sad. Instead, all I felt was relief.

I never spoke to him again. I didn't need to. I now belonged in the world he had introduced me to. I was no longer anybody's guest.

CHAPTER 10

"Cassie, your credit card is for emergencies. Maybe cool it a little," my father said through the phone. I knew he was right. In my first semester at Yale, I was using my credit card a lot. Yale was surrounded by trendy bars and elegant restaurants. Students flocked to them, and I, trying to fit in, did the same.

For most students, spending money wasn't a problem. The median family income at Yale is $192,000. Nineteen percent of students come from the top 1 percent income bracket, and almost 70 percent come from the top 20 percent. There are more students from the top 1 percent income bracket than from the bottom 60 percent combined. Only about 2 percent come from the bottom 20 percent. That's a lot of numbers just to say: Yale students by and large have money. They could afford to buy a drink or two every night.

In 2018, Yale estimated that it costs an average student $73,180 for tuition and living expenses per year. I was shocked when I learned that approximately half of my classmates received no financial aid to help defray this cost. They came from families that could afford to pay tens of thousands of dollars a year just for college tuition. There was no way my family could do that — the annual tuition almost certainly was more than our annual income at the time. Even with my substantial UWC scholarships, I still received additional assistance from Yale. My father joked that he was glad that "Yale thought we were poor," since it meant I could afford to go there.

Yale felt more privileged than anywhere I had been before. By that, I mean that Yale students seemed to have certain advantages other people didn't. A lot of aspects of life just came more easily for them. I had caught glimpses of privilege at UWC and Wellesley. But at Yale, privilege was the norm. It was pervasive, all encompassing.

UWC valued internationalism. It wasn't necessarily rooted in money — it was about how many obscure cities you had been to, how daring your travels had been, how many hostels you had slept in. At Wellesley pockets of the community prioritized money, but it was more common to value inclusiveness, almost radical inclusiveness. At Wellesley I learned that the spectrum of sexuality didn't stop at LGBT — you also had to include QQIA+.

But at Yale, students valued the privileges that our society so often holds in the highest regard: money, power, and connections. I know there were pockets that didn't place much importance on those things, but, in all honesty, those things were part of the reason I was drawn to Yale. I intentionally and doggedly sought them out. I thought they were necessary to succeed.

I had never lived in this type of environment, and I spent hours my first semester trying to decipher its complex status code. *Plastic purses for rich girls,* I typed into Google one night. I searched the images until I found one that matched, and I ordered my first Longchamp bag the next day. I turned to eBay for the things I couldn't afford. I bought a used Burberry scarf and a deeply discounted used Gucci purse. My stomach dropped when I lost the scarf at a party a few weeks later. Unlike many of my classmates, I couldn't afford to buy another one. I wasn't always successful at my attempts to decipher these hidden rules. I still haven't been able to figure out who makes the black ballet flats with the gold design on the toe.

Navigating Yale wasn't just about learning how to be comfortable around wealth. One of my friends comes from a well-to-do family in Alabama. But even he felt out of place when he went to Yale for law school after attending a state university. "It's like everyone else is playing a game," he told me years later. "It's not just that you don't know the rules — it's that you didn't even know there was a game being played." By the time he figured out how this game worked — network relentlessly, befriend powerful people, host and attend dinner parties — he felt like he was a year behind the rest of his classmates.

My parents did their best to support my newfound desire for overpriced things. They didn't understand it, but they wanted me to feel comfortable in my new environment. I cringe when I remember telling my mother, just before I ordered the scarf I would later lose, "You don't understand. *Everyone* has a Burberry scarf." That statement wasn't quite true, but it felt true then. My mother, ever self-sacrificing, told me to use her credit card to buy it.

When my mother was in high school, she was on the homecoming court. She was thrilled, but worried that she didn't have anything appropriate to wear. Granny knew, without Wilma saying anything, that Wilma needed a dress for the occasion. Granny broke into Papaw's money box, found a ride to town, and bought Wilma a brand-new one. It was a brown knee-length dress, and more money than they could afford, but Granny wanted her daughter to feel comfortable, even special, for the event. After hearing that story, I understood why my mother bought me the Burberry scarf.

Along with my new exterior, I added a twist to my interior narrative. People on campus were curious about the new transfer student, and it didn't take long for me to realize they lost interest when I started talking about a small town in the foothills of Appalachia. It sounded so middle class, possibly even poor. But not the type of poor that was trendy to take an interest in. I thought I saw their eyes glaze over as they looked for a way out of the conversation.

Eventually I began telling people the things I believed they wanted to hear. "I grew up on a farm in Kentucky. We had horses," I would say, hoping to conjure images of manicured fences and well-pedigreed racehorses. I never told anyone that the farm I mentioned was in a holler called Cow Creek, or that the horses were nothing more than old farm animals. They didn't ask too many questions. Most of the time they would laugh and say something like "Well, a real-life Southern belle, all the way up here in New England."

The Yale community valued intelligence, so much so that being smart could, in some ways, make up for a lack of money and social standing. I threw myself into my classes, staying up late and waking up early. I chose classes based not on what I was interested in, but on what I thought I could do well in. I earned good grades, and I think some classmates began to respect my drive and achievement. The better I did in my classes, the more I began to feel I had objective proof that I deserved to be there. I graduated from Yale with a perfect 4.0 GPA.

By graduation, I was pretty good at behaving like a person with privilege. I had almost convinced even myself that this was who I was. I knew how to dress for a cocktail party, and what to wear to a formal event. My residential college hosted a series of events for seniors designed to teach us how to behave in different types of social settings. Our final event of the year was a lobster bake with unlimited lobster. It was the first time I had ever had lobster, and I analyzed everyone around me to make sure I was eating it correctly. I felt as though I had, again, constructed a façade, an outward-facing version of myself that I wanted to show the world. It was important to me that it stay intact. In hindsight, I wonder how many of my classmates were doing the same thing.

I look at this, the impulse to turn myself into something I wasn't, and I'm a bit disgusted with it. Now I'm not even sure that this transformation was necessary to fit in, to be valued, at Yale. Even if it was, I wish I would've been strong enough to own my identity and roots, to recognize the worth in the ways I was different from other students. But, like a lot of people in their late teens and early twenties, I desperately wanted to belong, to have friends, to fit in. I wanted to be able to seize every opportunity available to me, the opportunities that my family had worked hard to give to me. I didn't think I could do that as just myself.

Yale felt surprisingly male. It's not that Yale didn't have plenty of programs designed to support and empower women. It did. Tons of them. And, as at most progressive universities, gender was a topic discussed frequently and thoroughly in the classroom. Those efforts, however, did not entirely erase the feeling that Yale was a place where men belonged more than women, where male voices mattered a bit more than female ones.

After my first year, I walked through a Yale spring reunion. I knew Yale did not admit women until 1969. So, of course, I also knew that all of the classes before that year were male — only it was different seeing it in person. The unbroken sea of masculine faces was a powerful visual reminder: for many years, women weren't welcome here.

But it's not all history. When I was at Yale a certain section of socializing revolved around fraternities, many of which were clustered on streets close to campus. Just like the finals clubs at Harvard, the male members controlled access to this part of social life.

I stuck around Yale for an extra year to complete a combined bachelor's/master's in public health. That year, the fraternities gained national attention when one frat made pledges march to the Women's Table — a fountain that commemorates women at Yale — and chant "No means yes; yes means anal." That same year the Justice Department began investigating Yale for fail-

198

ing to eliminate a hostile environment toward women.

I wasn't surprised. Many times I'd heard men objectify women in the dining halls. I'd seen them selectively allow women into parties based on their appearances. I'd had several friends talk to me about how handsy a guy had gotten at a party, and how he persisted even after the woman said she wasn't interested. Many of the women justified this behavior based on the man's drunkenness. "He didn't mean to cross a line, I don't think. He was just drunk," I heard more than one friend say.

I think a sense of entitlement was at play. It's hard not to feel entitled to things when the whole world tells you that you are. Yale students are told that they are the best and the brightest, that the world is their oyster. Powerful people pass through campus on a regular basis. I'm pretty sure I once saw Tony Blair and Denzel Washington in the same day. There's a sense of invincibility that comes from it all. And, if an institution — such as a fraternity — tells you women are among the things that are yours to take, you probably start to believe it. Years later, I watched my Facebook newsfeed fill up with my classmates' stories of "Me Too." The harassment, objectification, and assault at

Yale had been even more pervasive than I'd realized. In 2018, Brett Kavanaugh was nominated to the Supreme Court, and the nation focused its attention on the good-old-boys party culture of Yale. *Are people really surprised?* I thought.

I've talked with plenty of female classmates who didn't feel the same way about Yale as I did. They found it supportive, nurturing, a place of true equality. And I do think it's true that Yale, as an institution, tries to foster inclusiveness and parity. It's equally true that there are many good, thoughtful men at Yale, both as students and as administrators. But I also know that I'm not the only woman to leave Yale feeling as though this institution was not entirely a place for her.

None of this means that I didn't have an invaluable educational experience there — I did. I had the privilege — and, yes, *privilege* is the word I mean — of studying with some of the brightest students in the world. At Yale, I felt like the opportunities available to me were increasing every day. I began to really believe that I could go anywhere, be anybody, do anything.

My mother's world was expanding around this time as well. When I was growing up, there were few things that received as much scorn from my mother as alcohol. She was opposed to drinking, so we didn't keep alcohol in the house. Once, when I was a teenager, I found a few beers in the fridge. I immediately notified my mother. At the time, I was convinced some horrible human had planted them to make God mad at us. Now, I wonder if maybe my father just didn't remember to hide his leftovers after his Super Bowl party.

My mother's deeply rooted feelings about alcohol came from her childhood in Owsley County. There, alcohol use doesn't just describe something you do; it describes who you are. You are either the type of person who never drinks or the type of person who is drunk all the time. The judgment leads many people who do drink to do so in private.

Historically, there was also secrecy around alcohol production in Appalachia. Moonshine gets its name from the way it's made: at nighttime — under the shining moon — so that no one can see the smoke coming up from the still. The first moonshiners trace back to just after the American Revolution, when Scotch-Irish immigrants brought their whiskey-making traditions with them to the mountain hollers they settled. Moonshining increased in prevalence during Prohibition and the subsequent Great Depression because it was one of the few ways mountain communities could make extra money. They shipped most of the moonshine to larger cities, such as Chicago.

Moonshining began to decline following the Great Depression, but it still thrived in communities that had strict liquor laws. Owsley County was such an area: until a few years ago, it was a dry county, meaning it was illegal to sell alcohol there. Several of the surrounding counties were also dry, so the moonshine market remained strong. When I asked Aunt Ruth if moonshiners still existed today, she answered: "Why, Lord yes!" My father told me about a man who approached him in a parking lot a few years back with a mason jar and a conspiratorial smile. In 2018, law enforcement busted a moonshine operation in Louisville, Kentucky.

I've never been offered any moonshine myself, but that isn't terribly surprising. Alcohol has a gendered history in Owsley County. Young men were almost expected to go through a phase of excessive drinking, "sowin' their wild oats," as people like to say. Women were not given this leeway.

When my mother was young, one of her brothers showed up at high school "dead drunk" after drinking with some friends. Granny and Papaw rolled their eyes and sent him to bed to sleep it off. But Granny and Papaw wouldn't let Wilma attend any gathering that might have alcohol. "You can't be around those drunks!" Granny would exclaim. Anyone who drank was bad, Granny thought, but women who drank were *especially* bad.

Even though many Appalachian communities are dry, there is not a statistical difference between alcohol use rates in Appalachia and the rest of the country. Appalachia does report a lower incidence of binge-drinking than other parts of America, but the overall alcohol consumption is about the same. Maybe this is a sign that things are changing, that alcohol use is becoming more accepted. In 2013 Owsley County made it legal for stores to sell liquor. Berea still prohibits alcohol sales in stores, but in 2015 the city passed an ordinance to allow some restaurants to sell alcoholic drinks by the glass.

My mother retained her wariness of alcohol well into adulthood. Once, when we were at dinner, my father asked her if she would like a glass of wine. She responded,

"I most certainly would *not*," as she shot him a look of disdain. She was offended that he would even ask.

But as I got older, things changed. As my horizons were expanding, my mother's were too. It was as though my growth and change were contagious; as she watched her daughter evolve, she automatically did the same.

On one trip home, I told my mother about a wine-tasting class I had gone to with my friends. A few months later, she and I went to a liquor store and picked out a bottle of wine. She was so worried someone might see her that she insisted we park our car around the corner and dart into the store with our heads down. When we got home, she — after much hemming and hawing — had a glass of wine with me. Over time, we got to a place where we would have a cocktail on some of our nights out together. My mother, as it turns out, is a fan of margaritas.

Even now, though, she hides her wine collection from view if any of her family members come to visit. On Christmas Day, she will put her wine rack in the back of her closet until her family has left. Once they're gone, she'll retrieve it and open a bottle for us to share.

A willingness to indulge in a glass of wine

wasn't the only way my mother changed. She watched a Harry Potter movie with me and blushed when I teased her about not letting me watch it as a child because there was "too much devil in it." She tried (and hated) sushi. She drove back to college with me one fall and made her way through some pretty heavy New England traffic. The more I experienced, the more experiences she knew were out there for her to try. And the more she experienced, the more open she became to experiencing other things.

The summer after my junior year at Yale I went to South Africa. I had gone to Europe to visit some UWC friends right after we graduated, but this would be by far the longest I had ever been outside America. I had gotten a grant to study the attitudes of Cape Town students about gender, and I was excited to spend a couple of months in a new part of the world.

My mother, on the other hand, was not excited at all. "Cassie, have you read these crime statistics?" she said over the phone. "They don't just rob people over there. They break their arms when they rob people!" I could hear the genuine fear in her voice. But I was young and full of travel lust. I was not about to be talked out of going.

Finally, she tried another tactic. "Why

don't I come with you?" she said. "We can make it a vacation." At first I resisted. I was a twenty-something college student. I didn't need my mother to accompany me on my trips. Then I reconsidered. My mother had never been outside of the country, besides that one day trip to Mexico and a cruise that briefly docked in a couple of Caribbean ports. I was nervous about spending so long in such an unfamiliar place. It might be nice to have her along for part of the time. So I agreed and she bought a plane ticket.

I left for South Africa earlier than my mother to get started on my research. A month later, I went to retrieve her from the Cape Town airport. Her flight had landed early, but she'd had no way of contacting me, since neither of us had cellphones that worked. She was sitting on a bench in the terminal, her eyes darting around nervously. Her bags were tucked under her seat, and her legs were planted solidly in front of them. I had no doubt that she intended to kick any person who so much as looked at them or her. I could see the outline of a pouch underneath her shirt. She had asked me several times about the various options for keeping her passport and money safe. Despite my protestations — "Mom, you don't need to wear one of those pouches.

You will look like such a tourist!" — she had gotten one of the largest, most touristy ones on the market.

My mother stayed nervous for most of the two weeks she was with me in South Africa. But she didn't let her fears stop her from experiencing all the area had to offer. We rented a car, and she drove — on what was, in her mind, the wrong side of the road — through the South African countryside. I was in charge of navigating. When we reached roundabouts, we would go around two or three times before turning onto a side street, just to make sure she knew which lane to drive in when she exited the circle. "Yup, that's the lane," I would say as we began another lap.

Our last week there, we went on a safari. It was the off-season for tourism, so many of the guests at the lodge were local South Africans. One evening I came down to the common room to find my mother deeply engaged in conversation with the other guests. They were asking her questions about American politics and culture, and she was cheerfully sharing her thoughts on American involvement in the Middle East. From then on, we always had plenty of people who wanted to sit with us at meals.

My mother also made friends with the

staff at our hotel in Cape Town. She asked them about their city and took their advice on how to see it. She was open about the fact that she was outside of her comfort zone, saying, "I'll be honest with y'all, I'm real nervous about bein' here." On our last night in Cape Town the hotel staff gave us a bottle of South African wine and a dessert plate with the words *We will miss you!* written on it.

It was on this trip that I felt the relationship between my mother and me change. I was no longer just her daughter, the person she had birthed and raised. There was a shift in the balance of authority; we became more equal. We were companions, friends, joint adventurers.

I sometimes ponder this shift, how and why our relationship transformed itself. I'm not sure the relationship between Granny and my mother changed in the same way. Not because the two of them weren't close — they were — but because the older they got, the more their lives diverged. Wilma was moving ever farther from the hills, while Granny stayed firmly rooted in the mountains. They had their past in common, but their futures were increasingly different. There was something about the newness of the world my mother and I were exploring together that allowed the bounds of our old relationship to slip away, and a genuine friendship to emerge.

In the evenings on that trip, we talked to each other as friends do. She had begun working with children again, as a teacher for the Berea College Child Development Lab. This was her passion, and she was good at it. She had a knack for finding children who needed extra attention and making sure they got extra support. Teaching wasn't as lucrative as insurance sales, but it yielded her far more happiness. I encouraged her to follow her passion, and she in turn encouraged me to follow mine. I wasn't quite sure what that was yet, and we spent hours trying to figure it out.

I'm glad we had this trip together. It marks the last time I remember not having to think about her advancing illness. Her symptoms had begun a few months before we went to South Africa. She suddenly developed burning pain in her hands, feet, and shoulders. Over time, some of her muscles died. Her balance worsened, and she got tired more easily. The doctors were stumped.

They remain stumped today, even though her symptoms have continued to progress. The nerves in her body keep dying, and no one is sure exactly why. The doctors know it's an autoimmune condition, but they don't know exactly which one it is or what caused it. Her immune system is attacking the nerves in her body and brain. No one can tell us how or at what rate her disease will progress. The uncertainty is scary.

I might never get to go on another long trip with my mother. I hope I do, but her condition is unpredictable and I don't take anything for granted. Sometimes, when I think about her disease I get angry; it took my mother too long to be able to explore the world, and I worry that her ability to explore it will be cut too short. Other times I ignore her illness, as though ignoring it will make its effects go away. I've spent years searching for someone or something to blame it on: doctors, decisions, environmental contaminants, genetics. I've never found a satisfactory culprit.

My mother's illness didn't stop her — and the whole family — from coming to Connecticut for the weeklong festivities celebrating my graduation from Yale. For months, my mother had been telling me that she intended to be the last one on the dance floor the night of the parents' reception. She stuck true to her word. She even outlasted me, bobbing her head and snapping her fingers until security began ushering people out.

By the time I graduated from Yale, it felt mostly natural to be there. I had figured out the system, the code, the secret password into this world that had seemed so mysterious for so long. In some ways, I forgot that I'd ever felt like I didn't belong there. Although I still made the occasional faux pas — such as showing up to a Fourth of July picnic at a country club in a black business suit only to find everyone else in seersucker and plaid — I felt that I understood most of the rules and expectations of this new world.

But it's hard to inhabit two worlds at once. As I fit in more at Yale, I fit in less in the mountains. I didn't know how to be both of these people at the same time, the Ivy League graduate and the Eastern Kentucky mountain woman. So I chose to define myself as the Ivy Leaguer — it somehow seemed like progress, like an improvement in who I was. Like I had been upgraded with special knowledge and new features.

The Christmas of my senior year at Yale I arrived reluctantly in Owsley County. It was the first year I hadn't really wanted to come home. I liked being in New Haven, and I had a senior thesis and a New England boyfriend to get back to.

I entered Aunt Ruth's house in a black cashmere dress I had bought on a discount website, and I was pleased with how chic it looked. I wore black leggings, black boots, and a black headband with an oversized black bow. The rest of my family was in jeans and T-shirts, as I knew they would be. I looked out of place. Maybe that was the point. Maybe I subconsciously wanted to signal to them that I was different now.

I sat impatiently as we opened presents, taking note of each time Aunt Ruth interrupted or talked over someone. Had she always been so loud? It seemed impossible to get a word in amidst the noise and chaos.

That year my mother gave Aunt Ruth too many presents, just like she always does. "Oh, I just happened to have extra lying around," she said as Aunt Ruth opened up a series of expensive candles. "It didn't cost me much at all." I knew that was a lie. I think my mother feels a need to make up for the fact that she left Owsley County and Ruth did not, and giving Ruth a lot of presents is a way to do that. Once, when Ruth was at our house, she commented on a painting on the wall. The next time my mother was in Owsley County, she gave Ruth the painting and claimed she was "redecorating."

"Thanks, Shorty," Ruth said to Wilma with a soft smile. Even now, you can tell Ruth is the older sister.

I once asked my mother if she thought Ruth resented her for the opportunities my mother had. "I mean, don't you think she wishes she had those?" I asked.

My mother thought awhile before responding. "I don't think she sees a point in thinking about things that way," she answered. "I think she's happy with her life and happy I've had mine." I know that Ruth and my mother are still close, maybe even closer than they were as children. Ruth gets nervous about driving to doctor's appointments in larger cities, so often my mother will take her and Sonny. Ruth calls at eight A.M. most Saturdays just to chat. My mother knows nobody else would call that early and always says, "That'll be Ruth," as she reaches for the phone.

Still, each time Ruth asks one of us pointed questions — "What's it like in South Africa?" "What're you learning in school?" "How do you get to New York City?" — I wonder if she wishes she'd had some of the experiences we have. I sometimes think about taking Ruth on a vacation to Europe or California, but I'm not sure she would enjoy it. She went to Florida a few times to visit Sonny's son who lives there, and she told me that she didn't like it. "It's too hot in Floyida," she explained with pursed lips. "And there are too many people."

That Christmas in Owsley County, Aunt Ruth noticed that I was quieter than normal. She plopped down beside me on her couch and leaned over. "Honey, that's a real nice dress. I'd love to have me a dress like that." She brushed my sleeve in an admiring way. I don't think she actually meant it. I'd never seen Aunt Ruth in a dress other than her wedding photos and the occasional Sunday at church. I don't think she had a use for any garment that limited her ability to do chores and work outside. But I think she was trying to make me feel better about standing out — to let me know that even if I looked a little different, I still belonged with my family.

CHAPTER 11

I had barely gotten out of the car when I heard a familiar voice say, "Hey, Cassie." I turned around and saw Ezra, a classmate of mine from Yale. I hadn't known he was going to be there, but it was good to see him. We chatted briefly as I began to unload the boxes from my car. I had barely walked ten feet farther when I bumped into Kathleen, yet another Yalie. Kathleen told me that a third classmate of ours would be arriving shortly. I looked at my watch. It was eight o'clock in the morning. I wondered how many more familiar faces were yet to come.

It was my first morning as a student at Harvard Law School. I had just finished a year as a Fulbright Scholar at the London School of Economics, a year full of adventure and travel. I had roamed the streets of Morocco by myself. I had met the Queen of England. I had taken myself on a weekend trip to Belgium just to see what it was like to travel alone. I felt like law school was going to be infinitely less exciting.

The first time I took the LSAT — the standardized test used for law school admissions — my score was mediocre at best. That should have been a warning sign: I don't think like a lawyer. I like to live in the world of big ideas and unconstrained brainstorming. Logic and detail are not my strong suits, and I should've given those facts more weight.

Instead, I brought out my work ethic. I holed up in the library and pored over the pages of LSAT books. I woke up at six A.M. every day to take a practice test. I cleared my calendar for nothing but test prep. I blindly chased Harvard Law School like I had chased every other objective achievement up to that point. Eventually I raised my score enough to get admitted, although barely.

Of the 550 students in the incoming class, about a dozen of them had gone to Yale with me. There were dozens more who graduated the year above or below me. If I expanded this circle just one degree — to people who knew one of my friends or vice versa — a good chunk of the student body fell inside its circumference. Although statistics on this type of thing can be hard to find, one article suggests that 30 percent of the students graduating from Yale Law School attended Yale or Harvard for undergrad.

You would think that being a part of this cohort would have made my transition to law school easier, and in many ways it did. I wasn't intimidated by the fact that I was at an Ivy League institution. I understood the norms and expectations, and I was comfortable speaking up in intimate, intellectual environments.

But in other ways I was totally unprepared. Unlike a lot of my classmates, I didn't know any lawyers before coming to Harvard. There were none in my immediate or extended family. I'd never set foot inside a law office. I had no idea what lawyers actually did. I had decided to go to law school because I wasn't really sure what else to do with my life, not because I had some deep, burning passion for the law.

I didn't realize just how limited my understanding of the law was until I got to campus. "Are you interested in civil law or criminal law?" one of my classmates asked me at orientation. I hadn't known that the two were different. "Both," I said cautiously, waiting to see if this answer was acceptable. Satisfied, he continued, "Me too. I think it's good not to decide until you've taken classes in both."

Although I was the first in my family to go to law school, I wasn't the first to appear in a courtroom. When Papaw and Granny got married, they lived as sharecroppers on a farm in Sugarcamp holler, a few miles away from Cow Creek. But the Sugarcamp landlord evicted the family when Papaw, due to prior commitments, couldn't come help him with some house repairs one day. The landlord thought that since Papaw was his tenant he should be at his beck and call. The landowner arrived, irate, the next day. "You best be off my property by the end of the year," he said, his cheeks red, shaking with anger.

It wasn't hard for Papaw to find a new place to sharecrop. He was known as one of the hardest-working men in the county, and within weeks he had made arrangements for the family to move to Cow Creek. Papaw took this unexpected turn in stride. He had learned that life was unpredictable, and getting angry rarely erased the challenges he faced.

While undertaking this move, Papaw had his first and only encounter with the law. As part of relocating, he loaded up the manure from the barns at Sugarcamp to take with him to fertilize his new garden. Manure was a valuable resource on farms, and Papaw wasn't about to leave it behind. He never considered that maybe he didn't own the manure; he owned the horses that had produced it, and the food that he had fed the horses, so he just assumed the manure was his as well.

The landlord, known county-wide for his spitefulness, disagreed and sued Papaw for fifty dollars — the alleged value of the manure. When I drive past the Owsley County courthouse I imagine the scene: Papaw in his bibbed overalls and cap, explaining to the judge in his slow, accented speech why he was entitled to this particular pile of animal feces. Papaw insisted on arguing the case himself, in part because he couldn't afford a lawyer and in part because he believed that the law would be just and rule in his favor.

Papaw was wrong. The landlord won in court because of who he was and how much of the county he owned. He then tried to use the money judgment to convince Papaw to come back to Sugarcamp. "Come work for me," the landlord said, false sympathy in his voice. "I won't make you pay that judgment."

Now, Papaw may have been poor, but he

had pride — perhaps he had such pride because he was poor. And if that pride was wounded, he was forever wary of the offender. Following the lawsuit, the family stayed at Cow Creek, and Papaw refused to work for his prior landlord. Even though it was a struggle, Papaw found a way to pay the judgment.

There's a perception that the only way to succeed at Harvard Law School is to work inhumanly hard. Some of the most competitive people from all over the world descend on one place with the same goal. Unlike college, where there are many different, equally valid paths for people to choose, the road forward at law school is narrow. Everyone wants the same jobs, the same clerkships, the same spots at the most selective firms. There is a feeling that anytime you're not working or studying, you're missing out, falling behind.

I worked hard my first semester at law school. There wasn't much else in my life besides studying and classes. I would occasionally go to the gym on campus, but I tried to take my books if I did; I'd read my contracts homework while bobbing on the elliptical. I had trouble sleeping for the first time in my life. I would wake up at three

A.M., heart racing, and stay awake worrying the rest of the night. I didn't fly home for Thanksgiving because I didn't want to waste time when I could be studying.

My first-semester law school grades weren't great. Harvard does not give traditional letter grades, no A's or B's or C's; it stopped in an attempt to improve the mental health of its overly competitive students. But Harvard does employ a few categories to rank students, and, after my first semester, I ranked in the bottom half.

I took this blow to my ego harder than I should have. For years, I had defined myself by my grades. Academic achievement was a way for me to feel that I belonged in elite environments, and a lot of my self-worth was tied up in letters and numbers on a transcript. I had worked hard that semester, and my poor grades weren't from a lack of effort. It seemed that, for the first time in years, I wasn't going to be able to achieve in the way I wanted to. I moped in my dorm room for a week after grades were released. I was too embarrassed to see my friends, convinced that they would smell the failure on me.

But, in hindsight, those grades were among the best things that have ever happened to me. For years, blind, directionless achievement had let me put off asking myself some tough questions about what I wanted. Confronting those questions was scary, and I didn't do it overnight. But I was beginning to see that I couldn't be the perfect law student with the perfect grades, no matter how hard I studied. I slowly understood that instead of focusing on *becoming* someone, I needed to figure out who I already *was.*

It was in this context that I discovered the Harvard Legal Aid Bureau. It was hard to miss the Bureau students on campus. They were always in full suits or maroon hoodies. They always appeared busy, in a rush, and it seemed like they traveled in packs.

While most students at Harvard were engaging with the law academically — writing articles, working on law journals, participating in intellectual discussions — students in the Bureau were doing it in real life. Bureau students spend at least twenty hours a week — usually much more — working as real attorneys. The organization, a 501(c)(3) that is separate from the university, provides free legal representation to low-income individuals in Boston, and the students are the attorneys who staff the cases. They represent survivors of domestic violence in divorce and custody disputes, low-income individuals at risk of losing their homes through eviction or foreclosure, and other clients who cannot afford a civil law attorney.

The Bureau is entirely student run. The members of the board of directors are students. The executive director is a student. The president of the board is a student. Yes, there are supervising attorneys on staff, but these attorneys are hired for that purpose and no other — to provide instruction and oversight, not run the organization. That task is left in the hands of about forty young people who have not yet passed the bar exam. It is, as one professor called it, "the wild wild west of legal practice."

I applied for admission to the Bureau at the end of my first year. From the outside, it seemed like the Bureau was a family, and I was desperately in need of that. Plus, I was intrigued by the thought of helping people from a similar socio-economic background as myself and my family. I had spent the past several years pretending that I fit perfectly into the privileged environments I found myself in. Now I was curious to see what it would feel like to acknowledge the mountain roots and impoverished background I'd ignored for so long. When I got the call telling me I'd gotten in, I felt a peace I hadn't in a long time.

The best way to describe the Bureau is to say it's like being inside an Aaron Sorkin TV show. It's full of quirky characters, strong personalities, and bizarre situations. I spent most of my time in the computer room, where all of the students sit together to work on their cases. One afternoon I walked in to find a random dog barking (*Whose dog was that?*), Sam yelling about termites (*Why was he being so loud?*), and Chad muttering something about the constitutional law exam (*Had I done that homework?*). Steve, our token Republican, wandered through the room with no shoes, running his hands through his hair and muttering about court orders.

I became addicted to the Bureau: to the noise, the chaos, the fun. To the sense that we were all on a mission together, helping people who otherwise wouldn't get any help. We would sit on the front porch and laugh at how stressed the rest of the students were about homework. It was hard to feel worried about law school when you had a trial the next day. I was always busy, often exhausted, and, overall, happy. After all, I told myself, life was too short to be miserable.

I was in the Bureau's Family Law Unit, which meant that I represented low-income women in family court — a place I found increasingly bizarre the more I got to know it. It's still strange to me that a judge gets to make decisions about people's marriages, relationships, and families. The two concepts seem in such conflict: the cold impartiality of the courtroom and the emotional closeness of a family.

But I loved the impact I could have there. Nearly all of my clients had experienced recent physical violence, and most of them had young children. They were women in crisis, seeking to use the law to keep themselves and their families safe. I got to help them do that.

There was a steep learning curve. My first court hearing was a couple of weeks after I finished Bureau orientation. It was a protective-order hearing in a small town about an hour from campus. My supervising attorney, Verner, drove me to it. Verner had a Boston accent and believed in a "sink or swim" approach to lawyering. He didn't understand why I was so nervous to appear in court for the first time. He told me, "It will either go well or it won't. We'll just have to see." I didn't take particular comfort in those words.

When we arrived at the courthouse, Verner told me that he was going to go sit in the back. "You don't need Big Brother Verner standing over your shoulder," he said as he walked away. "Just watch what everyone else does and do that." I rolled my eyes.

My case was the first one called. *So much for watching everyone else,* I thought. I looked around bewilderedly and tried to find Verner. I didn't know where I was supposed to stand. Did I go up to the judge? Stand at the podium? Speak from where I was at? Verner, seated in the back row, gave me a double thumbs-up and a cheesy grin. I walked to the place from where I thought it made the most sense to address the judge: the witness stand. I spoke for a solid two minutes before the bailiff gently ushered me out. Turns out that the witness stand is only for people who are testifying, and lawyers never testify. My face turned bright red.

Verner had a cheerful attitude about the whole thing. "Well, you'll never go into court without knowing where to stand again," he told me as we headed back toward Cambridge. He was right. The first thing I do when I get to any courtroom now is ask the clerk where I should go.

I got better at lawyering the more I did it. I learned how to file motions and argue in court. I learned to subpoena witnesses and object to improper questions. I learned how to ask my clients about their experiences with violence in a way that helped the judge understand what they had been through and how it had affected them. I started to realize that maybe there was a type of lawyering I could be good at after all. This type of law wasn't about details or logic; it was about telling people's stories.

I saw a lot of my family in my clients. One of my first clients was a young woman named Fatimah. She had immigrated to the United States a few years before with her physically abusive husband, but had recently left him because she was worried about her child growing up around such violence. Twenty years old, she was going to community college and working full time to provide for her one-year-old son. When I looked at her, I saw my mother at the same age: a young woman using education to build something for her child, finding herself in a strange, unfamiliar place and learning to navigate it. We went to court to get Fatimah custody of her son, but a few weeks later she decided to go back to her abusive husband. I spent an hour with her on the phone, trying to gently persuade her to change her mind. But she wasn't ready to leave, and it wasn't my role to judge her. "I'll be here if you ever need me again," I told her before hanging up. "Don't hesitate to call."

Another one of my clients, Mary, was a young mother struggling to pay her bills after she had separated from a husband who hit her and their children. Mary wanted to get a full-time job, but she was stuck caring for her disabled father. She worried about where and how she could earn enough money. In Mary, I saw Granny as a child: a young woman who had to work twice as hard because she had to care for a disabled parent. The day I got Mary sole custody, she was so excited that her normally somber face erupted into a smile. She enveloped me in a big hug, then lifted me off of the ground and twirled me around. I had to ask her three times to put me down.

I also saw myself in my clients. We would spend hours together in the Suffolk County Courthouse, waiting for our cases to be called. After we had talked about the case for a while, we would fill the remaining time with casual conversation. Sometimes we would talk about the struggles they were facing in their lives, but more often we just made small talk. We chatted about the local news, celebrity gossip, our tastes in music.

In their backgrounds and stories, I could see the pivot points in my own. How a few different turns along the way could have led me to face the same challenges they now faced. How chance had played a role in me ending up in the hallowed halls of the Ivy League. Once I saw it — that thread of luck running through my life — I could never again ignore its presence.

"What do you want to be when you grow up?" I asked my second cousin Billy. He was around eight years old. I was home from law school for Christmas, and we were at Uncle Dale's house for the holiday dinner. The house smelled like baked ham and corn bread. I stood next to the wood-fired stove that heated the house, warming my hands after being outside to visit the prize goats that Mabel — Dale's wife — kept on the hill. This year it felt better to be at home; somehow my work at the Bureau had made me feel comfortable here again.

I was trying to make conversation with Billy, my cousin Melissa's son. He was a quiet child, always with his shoulders rolled forward and his eyes cast slightly down. Despite his shyness, I know that he's bright; he took the engineering kit my parents bought him for Christmas that year and assembled the entire system in about an hour.

"I don't know," Billy mumbled in answer to my question. "I guess I'll just grow up and get on the draw." I flinched with surprise.

He meant the Social Security Disability system, where those who qualify as disabled "draw" a paycheck from the government each month. I shouldn't have been surprised to hear him say this. He lives in a county where 20 percent of the population receives disability payments. His own mother had been talking about getting on disability for several years now. "My back has been hurting," she would complain too loudly at family holidays. "I'm not sure I'll be able to work much longer." Everybody nodded. It's no wonder Billy thought that the disability system was a valid career option.

"But don't you want to go to college?" I asked him, choosing to avoid a conversation about why getting on the draw is perhaps not the best life goal.

"I ain't going to college," he said with little fanfare. "That ain't for me. I'm going to stay in Owsley County with Papaw." By Papaw, he meant Melissa's father, my uncle Dale. Billy stayed with his grandparents for much of his childhood while his mother moved from husband to husband, house to house. I'd lost touch with Melissa over the years, seeing her only at the occasional family holiday. But Aunt Ruth kept me up to date about what she was doing, and I knew how different our lives had become.

Billy's comment bothered me; it stayed with me the rest of Christmas Day, and it distracted me from fully enjoying being with my family. Billy hadn't finished elementary school, and he had already decided that college was not for him — that he wanted to spend the rest of his life in this holler in the mountains.

I talked about it with my parents on the drive back to Berea, urgently trying to understand where his answer came from. I railed against Melissa during that car ride, declaring it her fault that her son didn't understand the importance of education. "If she would just grow up and go back to school — or even get a job — maybe Billy would see things differently!" I said with the blind judgment and conviction that only someone in her twenties can muster.

I wonder if Billy didn't think about going to college because he hadn't seen clearly enough what education could do. Experts on education say that exposing low-income children to higher-income environments is one of the most effective tools for motivating them to strive to do well in school. The argument is that if a child sees the possibilities an education can create, he will use education as a means to pursue those possibilities. Exposure to aspirational environments motivates students to work hard to create a better life for themselves. Of course, that process only works if there are better opportunities to be seen.

Up to that point, Billy had had little exposure to anything other than poverty. Like they had with Melissa before him, Dale and Mabel had instilled in him fears about the world outside of Owsley County. He couldn't go away from home because he might get sick. He couldn't play outside too much because he might get hurt. He couldn't try new and unfamiliar things because it might turn out badly. It was the old narrative of fear, repackaged for the next generation.

I wanted to sit down with Billy, that Christmas Day, and explain to him the value of education. The things education had done for our family. I wanted to tell him about Granny and my mother and all of the other women he knows who have used it to better their families. But for some reason I didn't. To this day, I still wish I had. Instead, I boarded a plane and went back to the life I had built for myself outside the mountains.

My second semester at the Bureau, I ran for president of the organization. I won, and I tried to use my role to expand our impact in the Boston community. We started a legal clinic at a homeless women's shelter, and collaborated with a homeless youth shelter nearby. We began a process that would enable us to take immigration cases of juveniles who'd been abandoned by their caregivers. I felt satisfied as I walked the mile home from the Bureau each evening. I started listening to Kentucky folk music again, for the first time since I'd left for UWC.

Of all the lessons the Bureau taught me, the most important was that I wanted to use my law degree to help people. I wanted to keep doing legal services work, to work with low-income people who couldn't afford a civil law attorney. The big question, of course, was where. There was a need for legal services attorneys all over America. I could do this type of work almost anywhere.

Most of my classmates were going to New York, Washington, D.C., or San Francisco. They were going to work at large firms in large cities, staying on a path that was clearly marked as prestigious. I was a little nervous to deviate from that path. I had worked so hard for so long for the right to be on it.

But, as graduation approached, I knew I was ready to go home to Kentucky. Objective achievements had lost some of their attraction for me — I felt pulled more toward the things that made me happy *now* than toward the things others said would make me happy one day. I was proud of my work at Harvard, fighting to make life better for low-income women and children in Boston. But I knew that people in the communities I grew up in needed the same assistance. And there were fewer people willing and able to do it.

My Christmas conversation with Billy had stayed with me. I kept thinking about him and the way he had already decided what his life was going to be. I imagined how it must feel to believe that he already knew the contours and boundaries of his whole existence. I thought that just maybe, if I was in Kentucky, I could do something about it. If not for him, at least for someone else.

I owed a debt of gratitude to the mountains, to the values and the people who had forged me. I was ready to pay this debt, to give back something in appreciation for the things I took. I had taken the lessons and the strength of the hills and left, rarely looking back. After years of wandering the world, I knew it was time to go home.

■ ■ ■ ■

PART III
HOME, AGAIN

■ ■ ■ ■

CHAPTER 12

I decided to drive home by myself. My mother and father both offered to fly up and drive from Boston to Kentucky with me, but this felt like a journey I needed to make on my own. It was a voyage not just to a place, but to a whole new phase of life.

I spent my last day in Boston saying goodbye to my favorite places. I went for a jog along the Charles River and had a pastry at my favorite coffee shop. I walked to campus and sat for a minute on the porch of the Bureau. I wasn't sure if I would ever be back.

I had gotten used to saying goodbye to places. My life since I left for UWC had been transient: I was always planning my next step to somewhere new. A decade of constant transition had left me tired. I was physically tired from moving, and I was emotionally tired from always saying good-bye. I was ready to go somewhere to stay.

But, as I hopped into my car to begin the fifteen-hour drive to Kentucky, I was also aware of what I was giving up in exchange for this stability — the way I was intentionally turning my back on many of the glitzy possibilities I had once thought I wanted. I intended to put down deep roots in Kentucky, roots so strong and winding that it would make it near impossible for me ever to leave again. Up until then, my adult life had been characterized by adventure, uncertainty, a lack of constraint. There was both good and bad in that. But now I was trading adventure for connection; uncertainty for reliability; a lack of constraint for meaningful relationships. I began to drive, knowing that the closer I got to Kentucky, the farther I would be from the person I was in Boston.

It felt surreal, going back home. In some ways I wasn't sure that Kentucky *was* my home anymore. And several of my friends thought I was crazy for going back. "Cassie, you love to travel," they reminded me. "You're going to be so bored, stuck there in middle America."

I reminded them that Kentucky did, as a matter of fact, have airports. "Some even with direct flights," I teased. "Don't worry, I'll come visit you in your fancy New York apartment," I promised. I hoped it was a promise I could keep.

Some of my friends had also come from rural communities. We had talked at length about the problem of "brain drain" — of promising young people leaving their home-towns — and justified our own role in it. Most of them now believed that they could be happier, maybe even do more good, away from their home communities. "National-level policy is made in D.C.," more than one person reminded me.

I was nervous during that drive down the coast and across the mountains of West Virginia. I sang along to "Take Me Home, Country Roads" at the top of my lungs as my overloaded car huffed and puffed through the Appalachian hills. I wasn't sure what my life was going to be like in Kentucky, but I was mostly sure I was looking forward to finding out.

There was one very important tangible difference between Boston and Kentucky: I could get a table at a coffee shop. I love working at coffee shops; I can concentrate better when there's a background of noise and movement. In Boston, it was next to impossible to secure a spot. I often got to the Starbucks near campus ten minutes before its 5:30 A.M. opening time just to make sure I had a place to study with an outlet nearby. But here in Covington, the city I had moved to, tables were abundant. The same was true with street parking. And reasonably priced apartments. Everything seemed just a touch easier.

I spent that first year back clerking for a federal judge in the Eastern District of Kentucky, the district that covers the whole eastern part of the state. Clerking is to law a bit like residency is to medicine: It's a chance for recent graduates to learn a lot of information in a compressed time period by working under leaders in the field. Clerks spend a year or two working with one judge, gaining a deep understanding of how the law plays out in real cases.

Many judges are based in a single courthouse. Particularly in urban centers, there are more than enough cases in the surrounding area to keep a judge busy. But in rural states where the population is more spread out, instead of the parties always coming to the judge, sometimes the judge goes to them.

Judges in the Eastern District of Kentucky have to travel, so their clerks do too. Although we were based in Kentucky's northernmost tip, every few weeks we would head east into the Appalachian Mountains. Mostly we traveled to preside over sentencings in criminal cases. Trials are increasingly rare; in criminal cases, well over 90 percent of defendants accept plea bargains.

I remember the first time I watched the court sentence someone for a drug crime. The bailiffs brought a middle-aged white man into the courtroom. His face was lined, and I could tell he was younger than he looked. The orange jumpsuit highlighted the sallow tones of his skin. His eyes were heavy with acceptance. He had been selling heroin to support his own habit. He had carried a firearm during one of his drug deals, and that act — as well as the amount of drugs he was distributing — had triggered a mandatory minimum sentence. He was going to jail for fifteen years. In the federal system, unlike in the state system, there is no parole. He would serve the majority of that time.

What struck me was how calm he looked, how resigned. He didn't fight, or kick, or scream as the guards led him away. He didn't even seem angry. In that moment, our judicial system seemed both very strong and very frail, as if the authority of the judiciary were based in large part upon people believing that it has authority.

I would see the same story play out time and time again during my clerkship year. The court had sentencings at least once a month, sometimes more, and sentenced two to ten people each time. A majority of these defendants were going to jail because they'd sold drugs, usually to support their own addiction. Many were also facing mandatory minimum sentences. Watching people file through the courtroom day after day, I came to know the face of Eastern Kentucky's drug epidemic.

I met Susie one Wednesday afternoon at a Starbucks near her home in Lexington, Kentucky. I was surprised that she wanted to meet there. It somehow seemed a little posh considering that we were getting together to talk about our Owsley County roots.

Susie, Aunt Ruth's step-granddaughter and Sonny's granddaughter, is about ten years younger than me. She and her father lived next door to Ruth and Sonny for several years. Susie and I joke that we were the children Aunt Ruth took it upon herself to help raise. Even though Aunt Ruth has always loved children, she never had any of her own. Susie and I laugh over the fact that she calls each of us by the other's name. I hadn't seen Susie since she was a child, but she had recently moved to a city close to me, and I was excited to catch up with her.

Susie grew up around drugs. She doesn't remember a time her parents weren't using them. Once, when she was seven or so, her mother left her in a stranger's house all night while she went out to get high. Her father used to give Susie drugs to hide in her socks when they were in the car in case they got pulled over. When she was in elementary school, she found her father unconscious from a drug overdose and had to call an ambulance. That was the first of many overdoses over the years.

When Susie was around eleven, her mother went to prison for several years on drug-related charges. Susie lived with her dad after that, and she says that he did his best to take care of her. But he was often high, and — even when he wasn't — he didn't know much about raising a preteen girl. Susie used to spend hours trying to figure out how to put her hair up into a ponytail. Although it seems simple, it's a lot harder when nobody shows you how.

Susie's peers had parents addicted to drugs too. But, even though they all knew about their parents' struggles, it wasn't something they talked about. They brought it up only when they were fighting, when one child would scream at another, "Well, your daddy ain't nothin' but a drug addict!" Families felt shame about drug use despite knowing that they weren't alone.

Aunt Ruth did the best she could to shield Susie from her parents' addiction. Once, when Susie was a child, Aunt Ruth noticed a bunch of disheveled, red-eyed men hanging around the house with Susie's father. Aunt Ruth, convinced that they were there doing drugs, asked the men to leave. "We ain't a-leavin'," they told her. "What are you goin' to do about it?"

Aunt Ruth walked back to her house a few yards away and grabbed an old board with rusty nails sticking out of it. She marched into Susie's yard and yelled, "I said git." She held the board up so they could see. "Don't make me kill you."

The men noticed the steely look in her eye and decided she just might follow through on her threat. "You're plumb crazy!" one of the men hollered as they began to disperse from the yard.

"That's right, I am," she yelled back, still standing firmly. "Git on to my house, Susie."

When she was in high school, Susie decided she was going to college. She had seen how rough life was for her father and mother, and she didn't want to stay in Owsley County and risk turning out like her parents. Plus, Aunt Ruth had been pestering her to get an education for as long as she could remember. Susie used to go over to Aunt Ruth's house after school, and Aunt Ruth would make her do her homework. No one else ever made her do that.

Even in the 2010s, going to college wasn't the norm in Owsley County. Susie estimates that less than a third of her high school class went on to higher education. She started taking dual college classes her senior year, and she eventually earned a scholarship to study nursing.

Susie's father promised her he would attend her high school graduation. He had wanted to go to college himself, but he'd gotten caught up in drugs as a teenager and hadn't finished high school. He beamed with pride each time he told someone that his daughter was graduating from high school and going to college.

The day of Susie's graduation, she didn't see her father in the audience. She spent a good portion of the ceremony hoping he would show up, but he never did. Later, she learned that he had overdosed that morning, and an ambulance had transported him to the University of Kentucky hospital —

the hospital associated with the college that she would attend in the fall.

A few years later, her father gave her a plaque that said A DAUGHTER IS A BEST FRIEND FOR LIFE. Susie checked the sticker on the back and realized her father had purchased the plaque while he was in the hospital that time. He had wanted to give his daughter something special to commemorate her graduation, but he'd been ashamed, lying there in his hospital bed.

That fall, Susie started school in Lexington, which is Kentucky's second-largest city. She couldn't believe how many people and cars there were. During her first few months of driving in Lexington, she would pull over to the side of the road and cry. She had never driven in traffic before, and it was all too overwhelming. She felt like she stood out among the other students; she was usually in jeans and T-shirts, while they wore fancier clothes. She wasn't sure how, exactly, they were fancier. She just knew that they were. She ended up transferring to a smaller school in a smaller town that she felt she could navigate.

But Susie was determined, and eventually she graduated with her degree in nursing. She moved back to Lexington and started a job at a hospital there. She got married and, when I met her at that Starbucks, she had her beautiful six-month-old baby boy with her. He had big blue eyes and smiled every time his mother talked to him.

She reminded me of my mother, this young woman from Owsley County who had set off to a strange place. The exact reason she had left was different, but the driving force was the same. She wanted something better for herself than the life she had seen in the mountains. Now that she was a mother, she wanted to provide every opportunity for her child.

Susie's parents still struggle with drug addiction. Her mother was clean for a while, just after she got out of prison, but Susie suspects she has relapsed. Susie's father now lives just up the holler from Ruth and Sonny, in a brand-new house that Sonny built for him. Sonny is getting older, and construction work is harder for him than it used to be. But Susie's father had just gotten out of yet another stint in rehab, and Sonny wanted him to have the best opportunity he could to start a new life.

The last time I stayed with Ruth and Sonny, we sat on the porch and watched the sun sink over the mountains. As we sat there, we could see cars pulling in and out of Susie's father's driveway. Each time, a passenger would get out and look around furtively as he went inside, then return to his car a few minutes later. We tried to ignore what I think we all suspected was happening inside.

Susie lives with the constant fear of getting a call that one of her parents has overdosed and died. She has to take medication for her anxiety, which she attributes to the ever-present worries she had when she was growing up. She learned at an early age that there is a lot to be nervous about in the world.

Despite all of this, Susie doesn't complain about her parents. She is particularly close to her father, who she describes as being "all heart." He once took the shoes off of his own feet to give to a woman who didn't have any. She maintains that he did the best he could to care for her, even when he wasn't able to do it very well. She is sure to tell anyone who asks that her father and the others she knows with addiction issues are fundamentally good people.

Susie wants to move back to Owsley County someday. She thinks there is a lot of value in going to a small school like she did, and she says there's something special about living in a community where people know one another. I agree with her. One of

Susie's friends recently ran out of gas in Owsley County, and three separate people stopped to see if the friend was okay. She had gas and was back on the road within minutes. "That would never happen in Lexington," Susie told me. "Even if you ran out of gas right in the middle of town you'd be lucky to get one person to stop."

She likes how the people in the community take care of one another. She was especially excited to tell me about a program that just started to provide every child in Owsley County with lunch during the summer.

But right now, there are no jobs for Susie in Owsley County. There isn't a hospital in town, and the one in Jackson — currently the closest, about an hour away — may close soon. Her friends who stayed in Owsley County struggle to find jobs. Those with a college degree do things like teach. Those without a college degree work at the Dollar Store or one of the two restaurants in town. A lot of those who haven't been able to find jobs have fallen into a life of drug use.

That day in Starbucks, I asked Susie what sorts of things she and her friends had done when she was a child. I wanted to see if her experience was the same as mine. It wasn't. Whereas I had the farm to play on, most of the farms were gone by the time Susie was growing up. A skating rink opened up when she was in third grade, but it closed down a year later. Susie thinks the lack of opportunities in Owsley County leads to at least some of the drug use. "What else are you supposed to do other than look at each other?" she asked me. "There are no jobs for adults and nothin' fun for the kids." And yet something makes her want to go back.

I had seen the beginnings of the opioid crisis when I was a child. When my cousin Melissa wasn't allowed to spend the night with her friends because her family was afraid of the drug use in the area. When the boys in my middle school class would raid their grandparents' medicine cabinets and trade pain pills. When young people started dying, and their obituaries in the paper did not list a cause of death.

When I was a high school student in Berea, we heard most often about meth, about homemade labs nearby being shut down. Sometimes they would explode and people would die. A recent study showed that dry counties, like Owsley, had the most meth labs per capita. It reasoned that an existing black market for alcohol made it easier to develop a black market to sell drugs.

But, over the next several years, I began to hear more about the pill epidemic. A wave of opioids entered the mountains in the 1980s and 1990s, as doctors began to focus on pain management as an important part of patient care. This trend wasn't limited just to Appalachia — rates of pain pill use in America went up almost tenfold from 1997 to 2002.

The pill epidemic hit the eastern part of Kentucky so hard in part because there was so much physical pain there. In Owsley County, more than 22 percent of adults under the age of sixty-five have a physical or mental disability. In Clay County, which shares a border with Owsley County, four out of every ten residents rate their health as being poor or fair, a rate that is twice that of the state as a whole. Plain and simple, Eastern Kentucky is unhealthy. It has higher rates of all prescriptions — not just pain pill prescriptions — than the national average. Many people began using pain pills to treat legitimate physical pain; from there they became addicted.

For others, the social environment likely played a role. A famous study in the 1970s, called the Rat Park study, examined the effect of social environment on rats' opiate usage. The experiment involved two sets of rats. One set was kept in a plain, boring cage, socially isolated from one another. A second set lived in Rat Park, an exciting and stimulating environment with plenty of toys and peer interaction. Both groups were given unrestricted access to morphine water.

The results showed that rats in the plain, boring environment drank more opiate-laced water than those in Rat Park. Even more interesting, when the rats in the boring environment were moved to Rat Park, they drank less of the morphine water. Although some have criticized the study for overemphasizing the importance of environment in addiction, the authors argued that their results proved that a stimulating, enriching environment impacts one's level of drug use.

People are social animals, creative creatures. If we aren't getting the necessary stimulation from our environment, we may try to get it from other sources, like drugs. And some parts of Eastern Kentucky don't always provide enough stimulation.

The steady supply of opioids into Eastern Kentucky helps fuel the crisis. In 2018, the attorney general of Kentucky filed a lawsuit against McKesson, a pharmaceutical distributor, alleging that that company alone sent 56.3 million doses of opioids into

Floyd County — in Eastern Kentucky — between 2010 and 2016. That translates to more than 1,400 doses for every man, woman, and child in the county. The lawsuit claims that the company either knew or should have known that residents would use some of these drugs illegally.

Today, some people get their opioids from "pill mills," clinics run by doctors who prescribe opiates without a legitimate medical purpose. These doctors profit from illegal prescriptions, often receiving cash payments from patients in return for writing a script. And not uncommonly, people get drugs from a medicine cabinet, either their own or a family member's. Doctors have prescribed so many opioids over the years that they're now easy to come by, even without a prescription. Opioids are so plentiful in some areas that they have been detected in the public water supply.

Evidence-based drug treatment — drug treatment designed around scientific principles — can help people kick their opioid habits. But this type of treatment is hard to find in rural Appalachia. There are fewer qualified physicians in any given community, and it's harder for residents to get to the physicians who do exist. Even when residents make it to a qualified physician, research suggests the treatment they receive may be less empirically based than treatments in urban centers — and thus likely less effective.

In 2016, there were almost 1,500 overdose deaths in Kentucky. Of these, 989 were related to opioids. And of the opioid-related deaths, 429 were from prescription opioids; 465 were from synthetic opioids, like fentanyl. The remaining deaths were from heroin, which many addicts turned to after finding they could no longer get opioids. In 2016, Kentucky had the fifth highest rate of deaths from drug overdoses in the nation.

As a result of the opioid epidemic, the mountains are full of children being raised by their grandmothers. In Kentucky, there are almost 40,000 children currently living with their grandparents, many because their parents are struggling with addiction. The majority — 83.2 percent — of these grandparent-caregivers are female, older mountain women who have set their minds to holding their families together.

I would see this effect on families later, when I began working as a family law attorney in rural Kentucky. Sometimes, I was fighting to keep children away from a drug-addicted parent. At other times, I was arguing that a parent had gotten their addiction under control, and should be allowed to spend more time with their child. Regardless of what side I was on, the courts seemed incapable of adequately addressing the many facets of these families in crisis.

My client Anne became pregnant during her senior year of high school. She suspected that her boyfriend — the father of her child — may have been using drugs, so she confronted him about it shortly after she found out they were going to have a baby. High and out of control, he became physical, pushing her hard into a wall. She got a protective order, had the child, and didn't hear from the boyfriend for months.

Then one day she was served with court papers from that boyfriend, requesting full custody of their son. Anne was determined to keep her child safe, and we fought to limit his time with the child. But the court system, with its presumptions of joint custody and shared parenting time, eventually awarded the father unsupervised, overnight visitation. He claimed he had been clean for almost a year, and he had stayed out of trouble with the law. Anne called me the day before the first visitation crying, genuinely afraid of sending her child into an environment that she felt was unsafe. It's still the part of my job that I hate the most, telling my clients that they should follow court orders they believe put their child at risk. A few months later the boyfriend was arrested for driving while high, and the court took away his visitation rights.

I couldn't wholly help every woman affected by the opioid crisis — and sometimes I couldn't help at all. One day, a young woman from Eastern Kentucky named Sarah showed up in my office. A child protective services worker had given her my phone number. "She's doing everything right," the CPS worker said to me. "She cares so much about her son." I had told Sarah that I wasn't accepting new clients at that time — that I had too many other cases. But Sarah showed up at my office anyway, her eyes wide with panic. "They're trying to take my baby," she said, immediately becoming teary-eyed.

Sarah had been in an abusive relationship for the better part of a decade. Her boyfriend used to force her to have sex with men for drugs. When she refused, he beat her. Sarah started off using pain pills, then moved on to heroin.

Social services got involved after Sarah left her five-year-old child alone for three days while she was using. The state took her son and placed him with her boyfriend's parents. Sarah hated the thought that the people who had raised the man who raped and beat her were now bringing up her child. She spent the next several years in and out of treatment. A few months ago, just after she got out of rehab again, the grandparents served her with papers. They wanted full custody of her son.

I didn't end up taking Sarah's case. I comforted her as she cried in my office, and I gave her the numbers of some other attorneys to try. I could tell that she loved her son and was determined to do whatever it took to get him back. I wanted to help her, but I didn't have the space for her case.

If I'm being honest, I was also grateful I had an excuse not to get involved. Sarah had relapsed several times. She had neglected and endangered her son when she was using. She had been clean only a little over three months. Maybe the grandparents were doing a good job raising the son, maybe they weren't. Maybe the rehab would stick this time, maybe it wouldn't. I didn't know what was the right thing to do. It all seemed so complicated. It still does.

CHAPTER 13

"Here's your stack of files." My supervising attorney pointed at what seemed to me an unusually tall pile of manila folders. "You have a three-hour hearing in Breckenridge County on Thursday." I felt my heart beat a bit faster at the news of the impending court date. "I can't go with you, but I've printed a cheat sheet of objections for you in case you need it," she added.

It was Monday. I had three days until my first major hearing. Somehow a cheat sheet seemed inadequate.

After finishing my year as a clerk, I received a fellowship to spend two years representing low-income women and kids who had experienced physical violence. Although I'd be based in Louisville, the largest city in the state, I would spend my time practicing in the rural courts nearby. I knew from the past year of working in federal courtrooms that women and children in these parts of Kentucky were struggling. I didn't have the skills to fix many of the problems they were facing, but I could help families in crisis navigate the legal system. And I could do it for free.

When I arrived in 2016, Legal Aid did not have a family law attorney dedicated to practicing outside of Louisville. In fact, the organization didn't *accept* family law clients outside of Louisville. This meant that individuals in fourteen counties had no options for free family law representation. If someone wanted a family attorney they had to pay for it themselves — regardless of how poor they might be.

The women I represented didn't necessarily come from the mountains. That first year of my fellowship I mainly stuck to the rural counties closest to Louisville, which fell just outside of Appalachia proper. But these clients faced many of the same challenges as women in the hills. They were dealing with poverty, a drug epidemic, a lack of access to important resources.

I thought I knew what to expect from working with these communities. After all, I had practiced in a similar field at Harvard. I had become familiar with the underlying law and the way it played out in the courtroom. I thought surely I was prepared.

I wasn't.

On some days I would spend four or more hours on the road, making my way from one county to the next. I used the time in my car to return phone calls to clients and other attorneys. I carried a mobile printer in the back of my vehicle so I could print documents wherever I happened to be. The printer always broke, though, and I got very good at finding public libraries. I joked with my clients that I was a one-woman traveling law firm.

Most of my clients were women, and many of them had young children. It was tough for them to find the time and transportation to get to Louisville. So, when I could, I went to them. I had to get creative with my meeting spaces: I met with clients at Dairy Queens, assorted gas stations, and a Subway restaurant. I would get there early to grab a table in the back so that we could have privacy from the other patrons. I would shoot people a dirty look if they got too close to my "office" space.

Sometimes I felt lonely traveling the back roads of rural Kentucky by myself. I missed the friendship and support system the Bureau had given me. But the loneliness was a good reminder: I was the only one out here doing this work. It was important that I keep doing it.

I hadn't been practicing long when Peggy's file came across my desk. What struck me most about it was the sheer magnitude of her poverty. Her only listed income was less than two hundred dollars a month in food stamps. She didn't have a job or any money in savings. I wondered how she survived on so little.

I met Peggy for the first time at a courthouse in a rural county. She was somewhere in her fifties but looked much older. She had long, flowing hair streaked with gray, and thick glasses that sat low on her thin nose. She wore acid-washed jeans and white sneakers, the kind with thick plastic soles.

She reminded me of Aunt Ruth when she talked. She responded to my questions with the shortest possible answer. I got the sense that she was always in a hurry to get somewhere else, take care of something else. It was as though she always had more pressing concerns on her mind.

I helped Peggy file for divorce after she discovered that her husband had sexually assaulted a young woman. He had begun acting strangely, and she found a loaded gun under his bed. He bought pigs, and she had heard stories of people feeding bodies to pigs to cover up murders. When she went to the courthouse to take out a protective order against him, she learned about his sexual assault charges. She was afraid of him, and she wanted my help to end her marriage in a way that would keep her safe. She couldn't afford to pay a lawyer; I agreed to represent her for free.

One of the first things I did when I got Peggy's case was ask the court to waive the filing fee for her divorce. Parties who want to get a divorce normally have to pay about a hundred and fifty dollars to help cover administrative costs. Courts must waive this fee, however, if they determine that someone is poor, ensuring that low-income individuals have equal access to the court system.

It seemed obvious to me that Peggy should qualify for a waiver. The filing fee was almost her entire month's income. This was a woman who drove a pickup truck from the 1990s and didn't have cable or Internet. She had never paid anyone to cut her hair. We put together the paperwork, and Peggy signed an affidavit stating that she couldn't afford the filing fee. I sat back and waited for the good news from the court.

The court denied Peggy's request and ordered her to come up with the money to file for divorce. I obviously was surprised, but I was even more surprised by some of the things the court suggested Peggy could do to pay for her divorce. My favorite was the court's suggestion that she take out a home equity line of credit to pay the filing fee. Peggy couldn't pay off any line of credit — opening one would put her home at risk.

Peggy was going to inherit a modest piece of property that was currently tied up in the probate process. The court suggested she just stay married until it was hers, and then she could sell it to pay her filing fee. But Peggy couldn't sell — she needed to live in the property after she divorced her abusive husband. She didn't have anywhere else to go. And, more urgently, she didn't want to wait to get divorced — she felt unsafe every day.

I went back to court, sure that I would be able to fix the mistake. I was naïve, and I still believed that courts were always in the business of doing justice. The judge denied Peggy's request for a fee waiver again; he still didn't believe that she was poor enough to qualify. I went back to court one final time, and the judge smirked at me from the bench. "This sure does matter a lot to you, doesn't it?" he asked, looking amused.

It did. If Peggy couldn't pay the filing fee, she wouldn't be able to file for divorce. She would be forced to stay married to a man she feared because she didn't have the financial resources to pay her court fees. This situation ran counter to everything I thought I knew about our justice system.

After receiving a final denial from that judge, Peggy and I appealed her case to the Kentucky Court of Appeals. As I wrote the appellate brief, I thought about the other women I had met who were in similar situations. I had spoken to several women who had the same trouble filing for divorce because judges would not waive their fees. I felt as though I was fighting not just for Peggy, but for them as well. I imagined the way this case would fling open the doors of the courts, granting access to all the women who had been trapped outside of our justice system.

We lost the case.

I could barely bring myself to read the full decision. I took it in one paragraph at a time, pausing every few minutes to let my anger subside. Not only did I feel like I had failed Peggy, but the precedent our case had set would also make it harder for all poor people in Kentucky to access the courts. I had thought I was making things better; instead, I made them worse. An older lawyer told me, "See? This is why it's dangerous to stick your neck out. The law is a slow and dangerous beast."

Peggy took it better than I did. When I called her with the bad news, she simply said, "Oh, well." I got the feeling that she had never actually believed the court system might rule in her favor. She didn't think that institutions of power were on her side.

Peggy eventually came up with a way to pay for her divorce. She rummaged through her garage and found a gun that belonged to her first husband, who had died a few years before. She loved that husband, and she'd wanted to keep the gun to remember him. She ended up selling it to a neighbor at a discount. It didn't seem fair, this woman with so little being forced to sell one of the few things she had. It didn't seem fair that the system had abandoned her to figure things out on her own.

I would see these financial barriers to accessing courts in Kentucky play out many times over my two years as a fellow. One of the ways that bothered me the most involved fees for what are called domestic relations commissioners. In some rural courts, judges choose to appoint commissioners to hear family law cases. This isn't common in urban areas, where there are specialized courts that focus exclusively on family law. But in rural areas, where family courts are not available, judges often appoint commissioners instead of hearing cases themselves.

The decision to appoint a commissioner isn't tied to caseload. I know this because I pulled the statistics from the Administrative Office of the Courts. There is no significant correlation between the number of cases a judge has and whether or not they choose to appoint a commissioner. It seems like some judges just prefer to avoid the messiness of family law, and they appoint a commissioner to deal with it instead.

The problem with these commissioners is the way they are paid — or, more specifically, who they are paid by. Unlike judges, who receive a salary from the state, commissioners are paid based on fees charged to the parties. Parties pay fifteen dollars each time they want to put a motion on a docket — i.e., each time they go to court — and then one dollar per minute for each hearing they schedule. In short, people have to pay the commissioner an hourly rate to hear their case.

At first it doesn't seem like a lot — a dollar a minute. It seems even smaller when you hear that parties often split the fee. That means my clients would usually pay thirty dollars an hour, plus the initial fee to put the motion on the docket, to have a hearing before a commissioner.

But for some women I represented, that thirty dollars might as well have been three hundred dollars, or three thousand. These were women leaving abusive marriages. Sometimes they didn't have jobs or a prospect of getting a job. They had no way to pay these fees. And these fees aren't a one-time thing. In contested custody battles, the parties will have several hearings, and each one may last multiple hours. It's not uncommon for clients to rack up fees in the hundreds of dollars. Commissioners are supposed to waive these fees for low-income clients, but I have never seen one do it.

My client Patsy left her husband after her daughter from a previous marriage told her that he was molesting her. Patsy's husband had abused her, but she had stayed with him for the sake of the young son they had together. Learning that he was harming her older daughter was the last straw, though, and Patsy left him and took the children with her. He filed for divorce shortly thereafter.

Patsy struggled financially. She hadn't worked outside of the home much during her marriage, mostly because her husband would get jealous anytime she got a job. "You're running around with other men, aren't you?" he would ask her. He would text her incessantly when she was out, and question her whenever she got home. By the time Patsy and her husband separated, she hadn't consistently worked for years. Patsy had large brown eyes that always looked a little bit afraid, and I wondered if it was because of the years of her husband's scrutiny. Her lips were always pressed together, as if she was biting down on them to keep herself quiet.

Patsy's case was complicated, and we went to court for a variety of issues. For the custody hearing alone, Patsy was charged almost one hundred dollars in commissioner fees. I saw her eyes widen with panic when I told her about the fee. She didn't have the money.

I got a charity to pay the fee for Patsy's case that time, but it still impacted her psychologically. Patsy was afraid that her financial situation would limit her access to the courts. She was worried that she couldn't afford to protect her child. Eventually, we reached an agreement in Patsy's case, and the court hearings stopped. But Patsy still lives with the anxiety that her ex-husband could drag her back to court and make her pay those exorbitant fees anytime he chooses. In custody disputes, you can never be sure that you're done until your child turns eighteen and the court loses jurisdiction.

Another form these financial barriers take is guardian ad litem fees. A guardian ad litem is an attorney appointed to represent someone, often a child, in a family law case. In heated custody battles, children sometimes get caught in the middle. They need an attorney of their own to represent their interests and be their voice in the middle of a messy he-said/she-said war between their parents. Since messy was the only type of custody case I took, I often had guardians ad litem in my cases.

Again, the problem was paying these guardians. Under Kentucky law, those who are seeking the divorce have to pay the guardian ad litem fee. In cases of domestic violence, the spouse who was the target of the violence is often the first one to file — after all, it is rare that an abuser will relinquish his control and just let his target walk away. In most of my cases, I was the attorney filing to initiate the divorce. So my clients were the ones obligated to pay the fee.

Paying these fees wasn't as big a deal in

urban settings. Usually, if I sent a letter to an appointed guardian ad litem explaining that my client was low-income and a survivor of domestic violence, the attorney would agree to represent the child for free.

But things are different in rural environments. Guardians ad litem are less likely to waive their fees — a lot of them seem offended that I even ask. Perhaps this is because profit margins are smaller for attorneys in more rural areas. Some of them probably can't afford to forgo their paycheck and work for free.

This leaves low-income parents in a bind. Often, they know that asking the court to appoint a guardian ad litem is the best thing for their children, the only way to give them a direct voice in the matter, to make sure there is someone looking out just for them. It can also tip the balance in a he-said/she-said custody case, providing an outside voice to give an opinion to the court.

But poor parents also know that they cannot afford this private lawyer. Guardians ad litem often charge close to two hundred dollars per hour for their services, even in the rural areas of the state. Many poor parents get stuck with bills in the multiple thousands of dollars just because they choose to provide their children with legal representation. Those who don't pay the accumulated fee risk being in contempt of court and going to jail. No matter how poor the parent, there is no mechanism for waiving this fee.

I know this because of my client Roy. Roy was one of the few men I represented in his divorce. His wife suffered from a mental illness that affected her ability to parent. Roy had been granted a protective order after she set fire to a shed behind their house while Roy was inside it. A few months later, she tried to run him over with a truck.

Roy defined himself based on his identity as a parent. He didn't have much money, but he worked hard building houses to provide for his family. He was a gruff man, but his eyes welled with tears during our first meeting. "My children are my world," he told me. When I told him that his kids probably needed representation of their own in the custody case, he immediately agreed.

After the first custody hearing, the guardian ad litem in the case sent Roy a bill for over a thousand dollars. I gasped when I saw the number. I had seen private attorneys in Louisville charge less. Roy made around $20,000 per year as a carpenter; he lived below the federal poverty level. He wasn't receiving any child support from his wife, and he was struggling to raise his three children comfortably.

The guardian ad litem wouldn't reduce his fee. Even after I explained Roy's situation, the lawyer insisted on getting paid. I wonder if he had just seen so much poverty in his county that he had grown hardened to its consequences.

I filed a brief with the court explaining Roy's inability to pay. It seemed unjust that this father would be forced to choose between providing his children with food and providing them with an attorney. It seemed crazy that only children from well-to-do families could expect to have a voice in the custody process.

Again, the courts disagreed. The judge was sympathetic to Roy's situation, but he was bound by Kentucky law. There simply was no mechanism in place to waive the fee. The judge ordered Roy to pay it.

I was working in rural Kentucky because I wanted to help struggling families. But, a lot of the time, I felt totally ineffectual. I wondered if I had made the right decision in moving home. It seemed as though no one saw the problems with the court system the way I did. No one else even thought they were problems.

It isn't just the courts — it's everything

about living in rural poverty. In urban areas there are multiple resources, both legal and otherwise, you can draw on to support poor clients. There are organizations to help people afford food, housing, fuel. There are nonprofits that provide affordable mental health care to adults and children who have experienced trauma.

But I often struggled to find resources for my rural clients. Most of the nonprofits that provide services are located over an hour away, and many of my clients can't make that type of drive. Some can't afford gas. Others don't have a car.

I didn't quite realize the importance of transportation in rural Kentucky until I started practicing at Legal Aid. Yes, I had heard stories of Granny and Papaw trying to navigate life in the mountains without access to a vehicle. And I remembered stories of my mother walking long distances before she got her driver's license. But I thought that we had surely come far enough as a society to have solved this problem — that everyone could navigate to the places they needed to get to in order to meet their basic needs.

I was sitting in court in rural Kentucky early one morning waiting for my case to be called, barely paying attention to the proceedings going on around me. This docket often took several hours to get through and, as an attorney who didn't practice there every week, I knew it would be a while before I heard my client's name. I wasn't one of the judge's favorites; he wouldn't put my cases at the top of the pile. I mindlessly checked my email on my phone.

A woman's sweatshirt brushed my shoulder as she walked past me toward the podium. The judge had just called her case, and she was making her way to the front of the room. I remember thinking how young the woman looked. She held a child on her hip, and her hair was in a ponytail. I used to tell my clients not to bring their children with them to court — it was distracting and it seemed like a breach of decorum — but I had long since realized that many didn't have another option.

The young woman stood tall as the judge asked her why she hadn't paid her child support. She looked him right in the eye as she explained her case matter-of-factly. She had missed a court date because she didn't get the notification in the mail in time. Her ex-husband had gotten custody of their child because she had missed that hearing. When the court gave him custody of the child, they also ordered her to pay child support. It took several months for her to correct the error and win back custody. She hadn't realized that she had been ordered to pay child support until recently. She now had custody of her child again, she explained, and she was working to pay the child support obligation.

She had first found out about the missing payments when the state took away her license because she owed back child support. Around that same time, her car had broken down — it was old and unreliable — and she had no money to fix it. With no license and no car, she had lost her job — the only source of income for her and her children. She was struggling to find a new job: She told the judge how she had walked three miles, with her children in strollers, to town last week to look for one. She wanted to pay the child support that was back due, but she needed more time.

She said all of this almost defiantly. I recognized that look in her eyes. I had come to realize that it often covered up a sense of shame. This young mother was choosing to be defiant in the face of this system rather than let it make her feel less than human. The judge just thought she was being a troublemaker.

I almost jumped up to help her. I was sitting in the front row and she was standing so close to me that I could see the color of her ponytail holder. But there were rules in court. I couldn't just pop up and start speaking on her behalf. I hadn't even talked to her; I didn't know if she wanted my help. I told myself that I would find her later, in the hallway, to ask more about her situation.

The judge scheduled a contempt hearing and told her to come back in a couple of weeks. He threatened her with jail time, and she looked afraid. My case was called next, and I rushed through the hearing, eager to find the young mother in the hall. As soon as I finished I ran out of the courtroom and looked for her, but she was already gone.

The spring of my first year at Legal Aid, I went to New York for the annual Skadden Fellows Symposium. We fifty or so Skadden Fellows are scattered throughout the country, working on legal issues that affect people living in poverty. Once a year, the foundation brings all of the fellows to New York to talk about their work. I felt invigorated, surrounded by so many bright young lawyers making such a tangible difference in the world. It was also nice to be back in a city, even though I no longer felt fully at home in that environment. I went to an exercise studio and worried that the New Yorkers would be able to tell that I was a tourist, an interloper in their city.

What I remember from that symposium was how difficult it was trying to explain all of the issues facing poor people in the rural parts of Kentucky. A lot of the fellows were based in large cities — New York, D.C., San Francisco. And with good reason — there is a lot of poverty in these cities and a lot of clients in need of legal representation. But the urban-based fellows' practices were very different from mine. When they talked about partnering with other nonprofits, I explained that many of the counties I worked in had no such nonprofits. When they talked about referring clients they couldn't help to other legal organizations, I tried to make them understand that we were the only stop for most of our clients. If I didn't take their case, they would navigate the legal system alone. I told them about one judge in rural Kentucky who refused to enter a divorce decree until after a client of mine gave birth; a local lawyer told me, "Judge don't want to be makin' no more bastards 'round here." Rural Kentucky is, I explained, a different world.

I don't think it's helpful to talk about

whether poverty in rural or urban America is worse. They look different, and they carry different challenges. They should both be remedied. But I was beginning to learn the unique face of poverty in rural Kentucky, and it was uglier than I had expected.

Constantly being around these dire circumstances was draining. My clients would call me on evenings and weekends, when their visitation exchanges occurred and crises most often arose. My stomach did a tiny flip-flop each time my phone rang. I never knew what would be on the other end. Once, I had to phone 911 for a client when she called me while her husband was assaulting her. Another time, an elderly client called me while she was having a stroke.

Sometimes, my clients just wanted someone to talk to. They were worried about their safety, about their children's safety. They wanted someone to tell them what to do, and many of them thought I had answers. "No, it's okay," I told one client who called me at ten o'clock on a Friday night. "I can step out and talk to you." I was wrapping up an evening out with my friends, but the young mother was crying and I didn't want to turn her away. I didn't know if she had anyone else to call.

I recognized that it was a privilege for my

clients to trust me with their children, their marriages, their lives — for them to stand silently beside me in court and let me speak on their behalf. But sometimes I resented this obligation that I had willingly taken on. My life didn't feel fully mine anymore. I was irritable a lot of the time.

"Can you believe I'm going to trial just to get my client possession of a dump truck!" I complained to a co-worker when I was working late one Friday. "A dump truck! It doesn't even work!"

But then, after the trial, I saw how happy my client was to have won this small victory, to have taken something back from her abusive partner. "I guess the dump truck was worth it," I told that same co-worker. "But Lord knows what she's going to do with it."

My cousin Melissa was experiencing the stress of family court in a different way. Shortly after Billy was born, Melissa had left him at her parents' house. She moved in with a boyfriend, and she didn't see Billy often. She divorced her first husband — Billy's father — and remarried. She went through three more husbands in the next six or so years. Melissa's parents — Dale and Mabel — raised Billy as their own.

Then, one day, Melissa showed up and said that she was taking Billy with her. Billy didn't want to go, and Dale and Mabel didn't want to let him. I wasn't surprised. At that time, Melissa and Billy's relationship seemed strained to me. When Dale bought Billy a toy car that he could drive around, Melissa scowled. She complained to Dale, "You never bought me the Barbie car I wanted growing up."

Melissa and her parents took the matter to the local family court. Eventually, Dale and Mabel agreed to give her primary custody; they got visitation with Billy every other weekend. Billy now lives with Melissa most of the time. He's gotten more quiet over time. Last Christmas he told me that he sometimes stays up until two or three in the morning, even on school nights. When I asked him what he did that late at night, he shrugged. "Play videogames. Be on the Internet," he answered.

I didn't talk to Dale or Mabel much about the custody case. I discussed it casually, but I didn't feel right getting involved. My views on Melissa had shifted over the years, become more complicated. I still questioned her choices and how those choices affected Billy. But I saw more clearly the ways that others' decisions had affected her. I'll always believe Melissa had a part in the situation with Billy and her parents, but I also didn't want to work against her. Although we found ourselves in divergent positions now — playing different roles in the same system — I couldn't shake the childhood feeling that, in a lot of important ways, we were still the same.

CHAPTER 14

Part of me felt at home in Kentucky. My work was always challenging and sometimes rewarding. On good days, I felt like I was making a difference. But this sense of meaning wasn't enough to make me fully forget the ways that I had come back an outsider. When I was finally done with work, I would go home to my small apartment in the young-professional section of town, and I would want to tell someone about my day: the way I had felt foolish in court when I cited the wrong rule, how honored I was when my client gave me a hug after the hearing, how nauseous I felt when a new client told me her story of abuse.

Most evenings I was stuck rehashing these events by myself. A few of my friends from Berea had ended up in Louisville, but they all had husbands and babies. None of them had much time to sit and talk through my workday. Even the rare times when they did, it felt as though there was a gulf between us. Many of them had stayed close to home, connected to one another for the past decade, while I had gone away. Over time we'd all shifted and changed. I couldn't just snap back into my former life like a missing puzzle piece. I now belonged to a different puzzle.

It wasn't easy to find new friends. A lot of people my age had lived in Louisville their entire lives. They were still friends with the same group they had hung out with in high school, and they weren't terribly interested in meeting new people. I envied these deep connections, these friendships that carried a sense of permanence and gravity. I had moved around so much that when it came to friendships, it sometimes felt like I had sacrificed depth for breadth. For a while, I wondered if seeing the world had been worth it, since it left me feeling so alone.

I thought dating might be the answer. I'd been single for several years, an intentional choice after bouncing from relationship to relationship in my early twenties. I had embraced the chance to focus on myself, make choices based on my goals alone. That path had led me to a place I was happy with: home in Kentucky. Still, I was starting to think that a life partner would be nice.

Aunt Ruth was one of the few family members who didn't pressure me to date. Every holiday she would ask, "You find you a man yet, Cassie? It's okay to take your time. I took mine findin' Sonny." She wanted me to feel comfortable carving my own path. Even still, she would add, "But you let me know when you git bit by that love bug!" She would pat Sonny's leg affectionately as she laughed.

It turns out most of the men I went on dates with had no idea what to think about a woman with multiple Ivy League degrees. When I told one guy I had gone to Yale, he responded with "Well, I could've gone there too, but I chose not to because the teaching there isn't that great." Another looked at me like I had just announced that I had a secret extra head. At the end of the date, he remarked how surprised he was that I had seemed "mostly normal to talk to."

I hit a low point a few months after moving back to Louisville. It was my thirtieth birthday, and I was alone. That part wasn't unique — I felt alone a lot those first few months in Louisville. But this was my birthday, and thirty seemed like a big deal. I had pictured a day of fun, friends; maybe a nice dinner out or a fun concert. Instead, I had dinner with my parents. We had a nice meal at a quiet restaurant, but it wasn't exactly the "end of an era"–type celebration I had envisioned. After they left to drive home to Berea, I spent the rest of the evening on the couch with my dog. At one point I put a birthday hat on her to feel more festive. She looked up at me with sad eyes and fell asleep.

For some reason, this loneliness made me think of Granny. I have always wondered if she was lonely. In her early life, she was surrounded by children and work. There were chores, and crops, and cooking, and cleaning, and countless other activities on each day's to-do list. She never sat still.

But I don't mistake activity for company. For most of her life she lived at least a mile from other houses, and she didn't have a vehicle to make a visit more manageable. She couldn't leave the children alone. All of her peers were as busy and overwhelmed as she was.

Who did she talk to in her moments of stress? Who did she confide her fears and anxieties in? She was still just a child herself, only seventeen when her first child was born. I wonder who taught her how to grow up so quickly.

The answer, I suppose, is no one. Like the generations of hill women before her, she was aware that life came with challenges. And she knew that ultimately she would tackle these challenges by herself.

Reflecting on Granny's life always made me feel a little whiny. I had family nearby who loved me. I was forming connections with my clients every day. I was even beginning to find friends. I didn't need a relationship to find meaning in my life. Like the women before me, I was independent. I had the fire and the strength of the mountains in my bones.

I decided, then and there, on my thirtieth birthday, that if I didn't find a husband, I would be just fine.

Three days later, I met Bryan.

I liked that Bryan was a lawyer, like me. I liked that he didn't feel the need to compete with or diminish my accomplishments — he was confident in his own. I liked that he wore jackets with patches on the elbows and opened the car door for me whenever we went out.

Bryan is a Louisvillian to his core. He was born here and has spent most of his life here. On some of our first dates he would pick me up at my apartment and drive me to a restaurant he liked, pointing to different buildings along the way: "That used to be an Italian restaurant several years ago . . .

that was a doctor's office." He knows the city, both as it is and as it used to be. As someone who had moved around a lot over the past several years, I admired his deep roots.

Bryan and I grew up a few hours away from each other, but our childhoods were vastly different. His father was a doctor, an obstetrician/gynecologist in private practice, who attended a lot of the births in town. Even today, people will come up to Bryan when we're out at a restaurant and say, "Your father delivered me years ago." Bryan's mother stayed at home when he was a child.

Bryan's father would come home from nights at the hospital with his car filled with new toys for his children and new presents for his wife. His family belonged to a country club, and they spent summers at its pool. The children went on international vacations and to private school. Bryan's parents were able to give him all the advantages I had come to recognize.

Bryan's extended family was in politics. His uncle had been the attorney general of Kentucky and the mayor of Louisville. He was respected in town, and everyone knew him. When I told people I was dating a man named Bryan Armstrong, it wasn't uncommon for someone to ask, "Wait, is he related to the old mayor?"

Dating Bryan introduced me to a different side of Louisville. We went to trendy restaurants, the theater, the opera. We attended charity events and galas. The contrast in my life was sometimes stark. By day, I would help a woman figure out how to get government assistance so that she could afford food for her child. By night, I would split a fancy appetizer with Bryan at a new restaurant in town.

I still feel uncomfortable about this contrast. I know what poverty looks like, what it means to live in poverty. I remember it from my childhood, and I see it in my work as a lawyer with low-income women. Part of me feels guilty for not being poor; I have a hard time justifying having or doing nice things. "It's okay to go out to dinner," my best friend tells me on a regular basis. "It's okay to take care of yourself." Part of me feels like I did something wrong by ignoring my roots — in poverty and in the mountains — for so long. Sometimes I believe I should reject any and all privilege to make amends.

A few summers before I met Bryan, I interned at a private law firm. Each summer associate got a stipend for meals. The firm wanted us to bond with the full-time lawyers, so they encouraged us to eat together. The dinner allowance was high — high enough that we could order almost anything we wanted.

At the end of one meal, the table was covered with barely touched plates bearing several hundred dollars' worth of food. I had spent the day fundraising for the Bureau. I knew that the amount of money on that table, in the form of untouched food, could provide legal representation to several survivors of domestic violence. It seemed like such a waste.

A few months after we began dating, Bryan arranged for us to go on a trip to a resort in the mountains of West Virginia. I had never been to a resort. I was used to traveling, but on a shoestring budget. The summer before I moved to Louisville, my best friend and I had gone backpacking through Southeast Asia. I insisted that we try to spend no more than twelve dollars per day on lodging, and I ate street food to keep down costs. My friend rolled his eyes at me in exasperation. "Cassie, I think we can afford to stay somewhere that has air-conditioning tonight," he told me after I proposed staying at a run-down youth hostel of questionable cleanliness. He gave me an "I told you so" look when I came down with food poisoning in rural Cambodia.

Bryan and I talked the entire four-hour drive to the resort. We covered everything from our childhoods, to our political views, to our favorite podcasts. He was easy to talk to, easy to be with. I kept finding myself staring at him a bit too long or laughing at his jokes a bit too much. I was decidedly smitten.

The resort was fancier than I'd expected. When we arrived, the concierge handed us a list of the activities at the resort that weekend. I looked at it and had to stifle a giggle. *Really,* I thought to myself, *people still do falconry?* I liked the romance of it all, but a small part of me felt bad about leaving my work to spend time in such an elaborate environment. When my colleagues asked me about the trip, I was purposefully vague: "We spent time in West Virginia," I said. "It was nice."

The last night of the trip, Bryan and I were walking through the grounds after dinner. We joked about how clean everything was. "Do you think someone sweeps the sidewalks each night?" I asked. I chuckled to myself, remembering that Granny did, indeed, used to sweep the dust off of the dirt paths in her front yard. Bryan laughed and we kept walking through the crisp autumn air.

A few steps later Bryan stopped me. "I know that I'm going to marry you," he said. "You don't know it yet, and that's okay. Take as long as you need to be sure."

I knew quickly that I loved Bryan. He kept his condo stocked with jumbo bags of peanut M&M's for me. My dog would roll onto her back as soon as he walked in the door, knowing that he would lie down on the floor and scratch her belly. He did some of his legal cases for free because he believed in helping people. I didn't need to choose which version of myself to be around him — the Ivy League graduate or the kid from Appalachia or the dedicated poverty lawyer. I could just be.

We balanced each other out. He reminded me that it was okay to do nice things for myself — that having a celebratory meal at a new restaurant or going on a vacation didn't make me a bad person. In turn, I told him about the mountains, the struggling families I worked with, and what we could do to help. It was a part of Kentucky he had never seen as clearly as I had. Bryan and I had taken very different paths to get to the place where we found ourselves. But, somehow, we had arrived at the same place, and we wanted to stay there together. Our backgrounds meant we often had varying perspectives on things, but our differences were thoughtful and thought-provoking.

I knew that Bryan loved who I currently was, but I was less sure if he could love the place I came from, the family that had formed me. I still remembered how hurt I had been when Diego judged my Owsley County family, and then judged me once he had met them. An irrational part of me was afraid that Bryan would do the same. But I was also afraid that they would judge him — that they would somehow see his privileged background and decide that he did not belong in the mountains. I didn't take Bryan to meet them right away.

Less than six months after our first trip, Bryan and I went back to the same resort in West Virginia. We had been looking at engagement rings, but he had made it clear that he wasn't going to propose yet. I thought maybe he hadn't had time to get a ring, or he needed time to gather his thoughts. I tried not to seem disappointed.

On our second day at the resort we went off-road jeeping. I loved the feeling of driving a powerful vehicle up hills and over the mountainside. It reminded me of four-wheeling or mudding in Owsley County.

Somehow, in the middle of this resort, Bryan had found an activity that connected with my mountain roots. He is good at that.

When we reached the top of a hill, the instructor told Bryan and me to switch places so that Bryan could drive. Bryan got out of the jeep first. He walked toward the overlook and asked me to come and look at some honeysuckle nearby. I love honeysuckle, particularly how it smells after it's been raining. I buried my face in it. When I turned around, Bryan was down on one knee. I don't remember exactly what he said, but I do know I said yes.

I took Bryan to meet my Owsley County family shortly after that. I tried to mentally prepare him for what was to come. "They won't really shoot you," I told him, "but they might act like they will. The important thing is to show no fear. They can smell fear." I was antsy the whole drive down.

I told Bryan the story of my father going with my mother to Owsley County for the first time. Wilma got mischievous on that trip, telling Orlando, "Now, if my daddy goes to get his gun, you just head for the hills and don't come down until it gets dark out." At first, Orlando was skeptical.

"Mmm-hmm. Sure thing," he answered.

As they got closer to the county border,

Wilma upped the ante. "I don't think he'll try to kill you, but he might shoot at your knees," she said with a straight face.

"Okay, Wilma," he answered with a half smile, "whatever you say." His voice sounded confident, but secretly he was beginning to worry. The counties they were passing through were increasingly rural. The signs of extreme poverty were increasingly visible. A pack of angry dogs had chased his car a few miles back.

A little over an hour after their journey began, they reached the Cow Creek turnoff. As Orlando carefully navigated over the holler's edge, Wilma saw her father pass in a neighbor's car. "Oh, hey!" she shouted, pointing at the retreating vehicle. "There's Daddy, right there in that car. I wonder where he's off to."

A few minutes later, they parked at the old farmhouse. Granny cautiously scurried down the hill from the house to the road. "Why, welcome, welcome!" she called, beaming. She patted Orlando on the shoulder.

After Granny had made an appropriate fuss over Orlando, Wilma asked, "Where was Daddy headed to in that car we passed?"

Granny, not knowing of the couple's

earlier conversation, answered, "Oh, he was going to town to buy shotgun shells." Orlando paled and swayed a bit on his feet. Even though he later discovered that Papaw was buying shotgun shells to shoot at crows, Orlando would never be in the same room as Papaw and a shotgun without being nervous.

Despite my fears, Bryan did great with my Owsley County family. He went along with Uncle Dale's jokes about hanging him from the telephone wires. He laughed when they called him a "city slicker." He spent time getting to know each member of my family. He and Uncle Sonny giggled in a corner, and when I asked them what they were doing Sonny shot me a look. "Woman, can't you see we are schemin' over here!" Bryan shrugged.

Uncle Dale kept telling him he couldn't be a part of the family until he "looked through the knothole of Mamaw's peg leg." Bryan looked confused and a little pale until he realized there was no Mamaw and there was no peg leg. Bryan didn't understand everything my family said in their thick mountain accents, but he rolled along with the spirit of the fun. "I don't know what you were so worried about," Bryan said. "They're nice people. And people are just people." As we were leaving, Mabel promised that next time she would make him a whole hickory nut pie to take home — she had noticed when he sneaked back to the kitchen for a second slice. Aunt Ruth hugged me and whispered, "I reckon he's a keeper." For a while, in that room, my past and present were together and getting along just fine.

CHAPTER 15

It was five o'clock on a Monday morning and Aunt Ruth was awake. I had spent the night on her sofa, as I sometimes do when I'm in the area for work. She always feeds me dinner; often she makes my favorite banana pudding for dessert. The second year of my fellowship I worked for the Kentucky Equal Justice Center, an organization that advocated for clients all over Kentucky. I made it a point to spend time in the mountains whenever I could.

Aunt Ruth came down the hallway that morning making noise. I sighed and tried to pull the blankets over my head. I knew what was coming. She entered the kitchen and slammed the drawers just a bit too loudly as she started the coffee. She was, in her Aunt Ruth way, telling me that it was time to get up. After lying there for a few more minutes, wondering if there was any way to steal a little more sleep, I sat up.

"Good morning, Cassie. You awake?" she asked, as though that hadn't been her goal all along. Her loud voice cut sharply through my fog of sleepiness.

"Yup, I'm awake," I replied as I stumbled to the overly strong coffee in the kitchen. Normally, I like my coffee weak and full of sugar. But when I stay at Aunt Ruth's I appreciate the extra caffeine in each cup.

There was no particular reason for Aunt Ruth to be up that early. Until a couple of years before, she'd worked as a cook in the high school kitchen in town, lifting huge vats of food and operating heavy-duty equipment. She liked that job; she got to interact with the children and sneak some of the hungry-looking ones extra food. She would make sure they didn't get in trouble with the cashiers by covering up the extra helpings of protein with bread.

But she couldn't keep doing that job. After decades of farmwork and two bouts with cancer, her body was broken in numerous ways. She kept working for several years just for the health insurance — she desperately needed coverage because of her medical history. After the Affordable Care Act was implemented in 2014, though, she was finally able to get affordable healthcare. She retired.

But, even now, Aunt Ruth still wakes up before the sun rises, looking for a task for the day. Sometimes, she mows her lawn with a push mower. When she's done with her own yard, she'll move on to her neighbors'. Other days she works in her garden. She has a list of older community members she checks on every day. The important thing to Ruth is that she works. I wish she would sit still a bit more. Or at least sleep in an extra hour.

People tell me that my aunt Ruth is a hard worker. When she's around for those conversations, she beams. Calling someone a hard worker is one of the biggest compliments you can pay in Owsley County. There is pride and dignity in work. For Ruth, work was also the way she could excel, be good at something. There weren't a lot of paths available to her, so she chose to be the best at what was: work.

In Owsley County, hard work is physical labor that breaks down your body: in a tobacco field, a coal mine, a lumber yard. These are the types of jobs that people know, the types of jobs that families made a good living doing. It isn't "hard work" unless it is physically challenging, backbreaking. Your body is your labor.

I understand this, the importance of the

physicality of labor. I remember the days of working in the tobacco fields when I was young. All these years later I still feel pride when I talk about those experiences. I was able to do it, this challenging work. I was a part of a family that undertook this labor.

But now these jobs have largely disappeared.

Some people don't understand the emotional toll of losing these industries. My friends from outside of Appalachia tell me, "Thank goodness coal and tobacco collapsed. All they did was hurt people anyway." They often follow with a comment about how tobacco damages people's health and coal is bad for the environment.

And they're not incorrect. The tobacco industry lied to consumers for years. It is responsible for the deaths of thousands of Americans. I count my own grandmother among its victims. Coal mining also has a problematic history. The industry stopped workers from unionizing, intentionally stoked racial tensions, and treated employees poorly for decades. Many of its practices hurt the environment, destroying the natural beauty of the mountains.

What is missing from these statements, though, is an understanding of the meaning these industries brought to mountain communities. Of course these communities wanted — still want — safer jobs. Jobs that didn't damage the beauty of their surroundings, that didn't put their families' lives at risk. But those jobs weren't available to them, so they took the ones that were. They were hard jobs, and the people did them with dignity and pride. A monument to coal miners in Harlan, Kentucky, honors those who "sacrificed their lives while supporting a family and the nation."

It's not clear what comes next for the mountains. The terrain makes it hard to move things — products, people — in and out. I was reminded of this on a recent trip to Harlan. Between navigating the tight curves and getting stuck behind several slow-moving coal trucks, it took me almost three hours to travel eighty-seven miles. I was running low on gas, and I didn't have cellphone service to check where the next station was. I drove twenty miles without seeing a single store or restaurant. This seclusion makes it hard for some parts of Appalachia to compete with other, easier-to-navigate places for industries like large-scale manufacturing.

In the digital age, landscape matters less than it used to, and many high-tech jobs can be done from anywhere. Jobs in areas such as computer coding, tech support, and call centers may offer a new type of career for Appalachian residents. But this would require redefining what it means to be a hard worker: engaging in mental work on a computer rather than body-crushing labor.

One company called Interapt is running a program to teach coding to retired coal miners. As some have pointed out, there are similarities between coding and coal mining; both require strong decision-making skills and complex technology. Another project is turning a reclaimed coal site into a solar farm. Although outsiders assume that coal country would be slow to embrace a renewable energy project, one of the founders says that the opposite is true. People in the mountains are eager to find good-paying, meaningful jobs, and they have welcomed this new industry, even when the Kentucky state government has made it harder for solar power to thrive.

It's hard to say whether these one-off opportunities offer a real way forward for Appalachia. One former government official told me, "I used to believe in bringing jobs to people. Now I believe in bringing people to jobs." He developed several industrial areas in Eastern Kentucky during his time in office, hoping to attract new businesses to the region. Now he believes that only the best-positioned Eastern Kentucky towns — those that are easily accessible to major cities via roads and airports — have a chance of developing. "That's the way of the world," he told me. Over time, he thinks that people will slowly trickle out of the mountains, moving to larger and larger cities until the hills sit empty.

I hope that he is wrong.

I'd known of Melinda Turner since I was a little girl. Aunt Ruth worked with her at the food service, and, years before that, she was my mother's middle school science teacher. Despite these intersections, I don't remember meeting Melinda until recently, when I told Aunt Ruth that I was writing about some of the incredible women in Appalachia. "Well, you best talk to Melinda, then," she said matter-of-factly.

When I went to visit Melinda a few weeks before Valentine's Day, her porch was covered in red and pink décor. She had even tied Valentine's Day–themed bows to the lights lining her path. "Come on in," she told me, greeting me with a hug. "Any friend of Ruth's is almost family." Her house was filled with beautiful artisan baskets, and the air smelled like cinnamon.

Melinda was born one county over from Owsley, just a few years before Ruth. Like most kids in Appalachia then, she grew up poor, even though she didn't realize it at the time. "We grew gardens, always had clothes, and were clean," she told me. "I didn't know we needed anything else."

Melinda's mother had been married to another man before Melinda's father, and she had a child from that marriage. When that husband passed away unexpectedly, Melinda's mother had to figure out how to support a daughter on her own — no easy feat in the hills of Appalachia at the time. It would be years before Melinda's mother would marry again and Melinda was born. In the meantime, her mother worked at any job she could to help provide for her first child.

Melinda's mother learned through experience that it was important for women to be independent and self-supporting. She taught Melinda the same from a young age, sending her daughter to work at a five-and-dime store in town during her lunch break from school. Melinda's mother believed that education was the only way to gain true independence, though, so she encouraged Melinda to go to college. Melinda started college at Eastern Kentucky University in

1975, a time when it was unusual for women from her home to go on to higher education.

After she graduated, Melinda and her new husband moved back to the mountains. They were both committed to improving the area they had come from and took jobs at Owsley County High School. Melinda started off as the science teacher and nutrition director. She oversaw the school food program and quickly realized how many hungry children there were in Owsley County. One child had never learned to chew properly because he hadn't been given enough solid food to eat. Melinda vowed to make things better.

She started by teaching herself more about nutrition, reading books and driving to conferences and working to get more choices and nutritious food into the school. But she also realized that her role wasn't just about nutrition — that she had an opportunity to make children feel proud of their school, of their community, of themselves. She started decorating the school for every holiday, putting up elaborate displays that changed frequently. People warned her that the students would destroy them, but she says she's never had a problem. "Even the tough boys like it when it looks nice," she told me. "It just makes the chil'ren feel special."

In a place where excess feels unfamiliar, Melinda went above and beyond. She bought a boy a suitcase and taught him how to pack it, after he won an award that would fly him to Washington, D.C. She made sure the school found the money to pay for the trip. When she encountered needy kids at the grocery store she would slip them an extra twenty dollars to help her carry her groceries to her car. She made an effort to mentor students and teach them about the importance of work and education. One summer, she and her husband drove a student to an internship every day of the school break.

Melinda kept working and learning, and soon the Owsley County school system gained recognition for having one of the best food programs in the state. It was one of the first to offer universal free lunch to its students, and community members said the school food service was "the best restaurant in town." Melinda went on to become the president of the Kentucky School Nutrition Association and, eventually, the president of the School Nutrition Association, a national organization. She was the youngest person ever elected to serve, from the smallest district ever to be represented at that level. In her role she traveled around the country, speaking out in favor of policies to give children access to more nutritious foods. She even testified before Congress.

Melinda's role as president of a national association with more than 60,000 members opened doors. Prior presidents had gone on to high-powered jobs in Washington, D.C., or similar cities, and Melinda had no shortage of job opportunities after her tenure. But she wanted to stay in Owsley County, near the community that she had worked to improve. Today, she has a senior-level policy job with a company based in Atlanta, but she works remotely from Owsley County. "I just love it here," she told me. "It's home."

As we sat and talked in her living room that cold February afternoon. I asked her what she thought about kids in Owsley County today. Melinda's role still lets her work directly with children in multiple school districts in Appalachia. "You're on the front lines more than I am," I said. She told me that she's worried, that she thinks a lot of kids don't grow up having the same sense of pride instilled in them today that they used to, that a lot of poor families feel more shame than pride. "That's not how it was when I was growing up," she told me.

"You needed extra pride if you were poor.

"But I also have a lot of hope," she added, her eyes growing more lively. "There are good kids with good values out there." Melinda sits in on one of the youth groups in Owsley County every so often, just because it makes her feel good to see the ways the young people support one another and the community. "Yup, there's plenty of hope to go around," she says.

Later, as I am driving home, I think about Melinda and the way her work breeds hope in the community. She gives kids the tools, both nutritional and otherwise, to succeed. But maybe most important, she gives them a sense of pride. That's something the outside world tries to steal from this community in the mountains. I'm glad Melinda has found a way to kindle it.

"Why, Lord a mercy, child! Jesus don't care what you're wearing!" I felt myself blush as Aunt Ruth's shrill voice carried above the hushed murmurs. I had a meeting in a nearby county the next day — Monday — and I had come down a day early to go to church with Aunt Ruth. It had been a while since I'd done that, and, without thinking about it, I'd put on pants before leaving Louisville. Pants were easier to drive in.

When I arrived at the church, I realized that I was the only female not wearing a dress or a skirt. I worried that Aunt Ruth would be embarrassed by me. I slipped into the pew next to her and whispered, "I didn't realize I needed to wear a skirt." She looked at me sideways. "You can wear anything you want to church." Her expression was a little amused and a little annoyed. "I like your outfit."

After church, we went over to see my uncle Dale. His birthday had been the day before, and I took him a camouflage hat and a card. His eyes got a little misty as he thanked me. He looks like a tough mountain man, but I know he has a soft heart.

A few Christmases ago he gave my mother an acorn with a ribbon fixed onto it. There was a story behind this handmade ornament. When Dale and Wilma were children, Dale used to walk Wilma home from school. One day, Wilma was bound and determined to find an acorn "with its hat still on it" to take for show-and-tell the next day. But all of the ones she found had lost their tops. "Please, Wilma," Dale implored her, "we have to get home. Mommy's going to be mad at us." But Wilma, fully absorbed in her pursuit, paid him no mind.

Because of Wilma's dallying, both children

were late getting home from school. As the sun grew lower in the sky, Granny got worried. She marched down the hill and set off down the small road that ran through Cow Creek. When she found her children loitering under an oak tree, her worry turned to anger. She grabbed a switch and waved it in the air. "Git on to the house!" she hollered at them. The children scampered to the farmhouse, and Granny followed behind, whipping their legs as they went. Dale was mad at Wilma for weeks.

That Christmas, over four decades later, Dale got Wilma an acorn with a hat on it. She hangs it in the prime spot on her Christmas tree each year.

Dale spent his life doing hard labor, first in the tobacco fields and later for the city water company. He dug ditches to expand the water system to rural areas. "We got water out to ninety percent of the county, I'd guess," he said, trying to hide his pride lest it be misinterpreted as bragging.

Now Dale's body is worn out. His back hurts most days and even his constant banter and playfulness can't hide his pain. A couple of years ago he gave up his work with the water plant to drive a dump truck because it was less physically demanding. He supported Donald Trump because he thought that candidate would make things better for him. But he just found out that his tax refund will be smaller than usual this year, and money remains incredibly tight.

That day after church, Dale told me he wants to apply for disability. He knows that he can't keep doing the type of physical labor he has been. He doesn't have health insurance. Even with the Affordable Care Act subsidies, he can't afford the premiums, and, even if he had insurance, he doesn't have the money for the copayments. Each day that he works puts him closer to a health crisis he can't afford. He drained his savings last year to pay for a back surgery out of pocket.

But Dale can't afford to leave his job. His family depends on his income to make ends meet. He knows the disability process can take years, and he doesn't have short-term disability insurance to help him get by in the interim. So each day he faces a Catch-22: He can keep working, which damages his body and undermines his claim that he is unable to work, or he can leave his job, which would make it impossible for him to provide for his family.

We talk about all of this as we sit on his front porch, the sounds of wind chimes and birds filling the pauses in our conversation. "It's not that I've had a bad life," he tells me, looking earnestly into my eyes. "It's just that I keep thinking at some point life has to get easier."

Dale wants to use the disability system for respite from a life of hard work. Many people in Owsley County do the same. But you don't hear about those stories as often as you hear about the people who use the disability system to avoid work. Such abuse certainly does occur — my cousin Billy wouldn't think of growing up to be on the draw as a legitimate career option if it didn't.

And disability isn't the only program people abuse. Once, before I went to the store, my aunt Ruth reminded me not to buy milk from a stranger in the parking lot. The federal government's Women, Infants, and Children (WIC) program provides milk to many low-income families for free, and some families need the money from selling that milk more than they need the milk itself. Sometimes they use the proceeds from these sales to buy drugs, and sometimes people just need the money because there are no jobs and they don't know what else to do.

My family received WIC for as long as we

were eligible, and we were on food stamps for part of my childhood. At some point, my mother chose to stop getting food stamps even though we still qualified for them. She wanted to be able to provide for her family herself, even if it was a struggle. Susie, too, grew up on food stamps. These programs help families in need.

One of my New York friends recently informed me, "You know, there's no reason for people in Eastern Kentucky to work. They can exploit the social programs to make a living that's better than a minimum wage job!" I'm not denying that there is some truth in her statement — that some people in Eastern Kentucky do purposefully and intentionally work the system.

But, as I reminded my friend, children in Eastern Kentucky aren't born wanting a life of fraud and deception. There's not some insidious "fraud gene" in our DNA. Most people, if given the opportunity to engage in meaningful work that pays a living wage, want to work. It's who we are, what our families have taught us to value. The woman standing in the parking lot, sweating on the hot concrete, trying to sell a gallon of milk for a dollar or two may — if you look at her in the right light — be evidence of that.

In 2018, my mother went on long-term

disability. Her doctors told her she should quit working. The nerves in her body were dying, and she was in pain. On bad days, the pain was exhausting. Her current job was demanding, and she needed more rest than it allowed. She hid her condition well — always putting on a smile and summoning energy to get things done — but the disease kept progressing.

My mother loved her work. That was part of the reason she was reluctant to leave it. She had worked her way up at the Child Development Lab, eventually becoming its director. She was good at it. People called her the baby whisperer because she could so naturally and easily calm an upset child. She supervised the Berea College students who worked there, and she encouraged the struggling ones to finish their education. She once bought a young mother's textbooks for her, since the woman couldn't afford to buy them herself.

My mother was affectionately known by families and children at the Lab as "Miss Wilma," the woman who always had a kind word and an encouraging smile. All of the kids at the Lab were "her kids." She put in long hours to make sure the Lab — and its families — had everything they needed.

I tried to have conversations with her

about taking care of herself, her health. She responded by saying, "I've been working since I was a child. I can't imagine not working. I'm not ready to not work yet." I would get frustrated with her, telling her that she needed to take it easy. She resisted leaving her job not just because she loved doing the work she was doing, but also because she valued work itself.

Part of this attitude comes from within the mountains. Where hard work is important, and good people work even when they can't. Where sickness and illness and disability don't stop you from doing what it takes to make ends meet.

But part of it also comes from outside the mountains — from the stereotype that mountain people are nothing but lazy hillbillies. This stereotype makes us feel ashamed: ashamed of our roots and our culture; ashamed that what we've contributed maybe hasn't been valuable enough. I think this shame is at least part of the reason that my mother continued to work for so long. She wanted to avoid falling into someone else's concept of a person "on the draw."

I was sitting with Aunt Ruth in her kitchen, telling her that people across America were becoming interested in these parts of the Appalachian Mountains. I told her about the books and the articles and the national debate about mountain communities like hers. One book, a *New York Times* bestseller, was set just one county over, I said. I doubt she's ever read *The New York Times* or knows what its bestseller list is. But she seemed to get the sentiment.

The first expression to flash across her face was pride: She was proud to have the spotlight shine on her community. She often feels like the rest of the world doesn't notice that she exists. That flash was quickly replaced by something akin to annoyance. "I bet they just call us a bunch of old hillbillies," she said.

I confirmed that she is right, that the term *hillbilly* is thrown around loosely and descriptively. I asked her what she thinks about it. "Well, a lot of people 'round here use it," she said thoughtfully, "and I don't mind it when people in these parts use it."

She paused and pursed her lips. "But I don't like them Hollywood types and New Yorkers usin' it," she said. "All they do is look down on hill people and make fun of us. I'm tired of being judged by 'em." She ended this thought with three emphatic shakes of her head.

She's right, I thought. Much of the coverage of Appalachia has portrayed the area as lazy, violent, incapable of contributing to its own rescue. But I'm not going to tell her that. She already feels marginalized enough.

Instead, I asked her what she thinks the word *hillbilly* means. She looked at me and tilted her head, as if she'd never thought about this particular question.

"I suppose hill people," she said slowly. "People that live in the mountains and cling to the old ways."

"What are the old ways?" I asked.

"You know, people that don't like real modern stuff. Like Junior Barrett. He don't want no bathroom in his house. Says the Good Lord didn't intend for that kind of business to be taking place inside the home." She chuckled at Junior's biblical sensibilities.

"But people don't have to cling to the old ways that much to be a hillbilly," she continued. "Sometimes people just like things done the old way. The way it used to be. Them people are hillbillies. There ain't nothing wrong with clinging to the old ways."

I wondered whether doing things the "old way" was always a choice or whether circumstances sometimes left it as the only option. Modernity sometimes chooses to stop short of this holler in the mountains. The NO SERVICE that appears on my cellphone the moment I cross the county line is a reminder of that boundary.

Once, a male colleague asked me, "If life in the mountains is so hard, why don't we just pay people to go somewhere else?"

I believe that the mountains are worth saving. People here work hard, care about their families, are surrounded by natural beauty. They are connected to the land and to one another in a deep and meaningful way. There are unique values and strengths in mountain communities.

That's not to say that we shouldn't provide opportunities for those who wish to go elsewhere to do so — we should ensure that those in the mountains have the same mobility as those anywhere else. But we should also invest the resources to make sure that those who wish to stay can live meaningful, productive lives. Young people are the biggest export of the mountains. Many leave not because they want to, but because there are no opportunities in the communities they grew up in.

"Are you a hillbilly?" I continued my conversation with Aunt Ruth.

"I suppose. In some ways." I don't disagree with her. Even today, Aunt Ruth doesn't have a cellphone or an email address. She's never logged on to Facebook and hasn't heard of Instagram. I'm not sure she's ever even used a computer. Her existence is very much removed from the tech-heavy hustle-bustle of the world today.

"Am I a hillbilly?" I inquired.

She tilted her head as she pondered the question. "You used to be," she said. "You're not anymore."

I was torn by her answer. There is a part of me that wants nothing more than to be connected to my family's history, to the way of life that they lived in the mountains. As a young child, I felt this connection. But over time I've come to feel more like a grateful visitor than a true resident, like a child coming home from college for the holiday break.

"But," she continued, "you still got a piece of hillbilly in your heart."

I felt myself swell with pride.

Chapter 16

I met Jeanette at the courthouse. I had a busy day that day, with multiple cases in front of multiple judges. I had told her to stop by sometime between nine and eleven A.M. and to look for the short strawberry blonde running frantically between courtrooms. When I arrived at the courthouse at eight A.M., she was already waiting for me. She was eager to get on with her life.

Jeanette had short brown hair and big brown eyes. She held her hands clasped in front of her as though she was ready to push away the world if she needed to. She smiled a lot, but her smile was tight with tension, as if someone were pulling up the corners of her mouth with an invisible string. She didn't smile with her eyes.

The bailiffs in the courthouse knew me, and they unlocked the small conference room just outside the courtroom so we could meet in private. Seated under the faintly humming fluorescent lights, Jeanette began to tell me her story.

Jeanette's husband, Mike, had always been a mean drunk. Sometimes, after he'd had a few drinks, he would come home and push Jeanette around. A couple of times, he hit her. Jeanette told me that he was always sorry after the violence, that he always promised to do better. I had seen that cycle play out many times before.

The final straw came one day in the summer of 2016. Mike came home drunk after an evening out with friends. Jeanette was lying on the couch, resting after a long day at work. She was half asleep when he began insisting that she make him dinner. Jeanette refused. She was too tired to be bossed around, and she told Mike that he was perfectly capable of making his own dinner.

Mike dragged Jeanette from the couch in a drunken rage. His face was red and his eyes were wild. Mike took her to the bathroom and began to beat her, hitting her head and face. At one point he wrapped a towel around her neck and began to choke her. Their son, Josh, heard the noise and came into the bathroom. He tried to pull Mike off Jeanette, and Mike flung him to the ground.

While Josh ran to get the phone to call

911, Mike pushed Jeanette into the shower and turned on the cold water. She told me that as she lay there on the shower floor, she knew she was going to die. She looked up at Mike and saw that he had a gun. He raised it, pointed it at her, and fired. Jeanette heard the explosion of the shot echo throughout the bathroom.

The bullet missed her.

The shot cut through Jeanette's clothes and embedded itself in the wall. Even today, Jeanette's clothes are still in police custody to preserve the bullet hole from that night.

There must've been something about firing the gun that snapped Mike out of his rage. Maybe Jeanette screamed. Maybe he had surprised himself with how far he had let his anger take him. Maybe he was worried that the police were on their way. The reason he stopped his assault isn't the important thing; the important thing is that he stopped.

Mike fled. He hopped into his vehicle and tore out of the driveway, minutes before first responders arrived. He must've been trying to make a run for it: He cleared out the couple's bank account, leaving Jeanette with no money and no way of getting any. It was several days before police apprehended him in a nearby county.

It was hard for me to look at the pictures of Jeanette's injuries. She had brought them with her that day to the courthouse, and she pushed them across the table toward me with little fanfare. I had gotten good at maintaining a neutral face when talking to clients, but these pictures made me flinch. They showed inch by inch the damage that Mike had inflicted upon her body — a horrific collage of dark purple, bright red, and faded yellow.

When Jeanette told me "I want to divorce him," I wasn't sure I believed her. Not because of anything about her, but because of my experience working with other clients. The assault had happened very recently, and I wondered if she was truly committed to leaving for good this time. I had known many women who started the divorce process after an assault and later changed their minds. It was the part of the cycle of violence that broke my heart the most: watching women I cared about go back into situations that I believed were unsafe. But I had learned some time ago that my job was not to make decisions about my clients' lives. Many of them had few choices in their lives as it was; it wasn't up to me to further diminish the options available to them.

But I should have believed Jeanette that

day — I should've seen her determination. Her gaze was solid and unwavering as she told me each detail of her story. Some women cry when they tell me they are ready to finally end their marriage. There were no tears in Jeanette's eyes. All I saw there was a calm, steady resolve. And perhaps a bit of impatience. She was ready to get on with things.

We filled out her divorce paperwork that day, and I told her that we would have a court hearing on some procedural things in a couple of weeks. "You don't need to be there," I explained. "It's just going to be about some technical legal stuff." Most of my clients are grateful when they don't have to come to court. Jeanette let me know that she would attend that hearing, and every other hearing. She wanted to be there just in case Mike was there. She wanted him to see her, sitting in the courtroom.

The first time Jeanette had to see Mike was at her protective order hearing. Mike was being held in jail for criminal charges related to the assault, but I wanted to get her a civil protective order to further limit his ability to contact her. I stood in between Mike and Jeanette at the hearing. I was struck by how normal he looked. I had been representing domestic violence survivors for a while at that point, and I had seen many perpetrators of violence. Part of me still expected them to look different, to show some outward sign that they were capable of the violence they had rained down. Mike didn't look violent standing there in his orange jumpsuit. They rarely do.

I was also struck by how calm Jeanette was, as she stood a few feet away from him. She looked straight ahead at the judge the entire time. She didn't glance over toward Mike once. After the hearing was over, she and I went out into the hallway to talk. She exhaled deeply, and her body deflated. She had braced herself during the hearing.

The court granted Jeanette's request for a protective order, and her case continued to progress. The next step was for the court to appoint an attorney to represent Mike, who remained in jail on criminal charges. Many people believe that you have a right to representation in all court cases. Most of us have seen enough legal shows to memorize the portion of the Miranda warnings that says, "You have the right to an attorney. If you cannot afford an attorney, one will be provided to you free of charge." What most people don't realize, though, is that this safeguard applies only to criminal cases — there is no blanket guarantee of an attorney in civil cases. That is true even though civil law impacts some of the most important interests in society, including our children and our families.

There are, however, a few types of cases where the right to a civil law attorney is guaranteed. One such case in Kentucky is when a person is incarcerated. If someone is in jail, the court must appoint that person an attorney before it can enter any kind of judgment — including a judgment of divorce — against him or her. This law is based on the idea that prisoners are wards of the state and deserve extra protection to make sure their rights are not violated while the state has custody of them. Public defenders aren't an option for these cases, since they usually take only criminal cases. That means the court must appoint a private attorney to represent the incarcerated spouse.

When I first explained all of this to Jeanette, she looked surprised. "You mean to tell me that he gets a lawyer? Even though I can't afford a lawyer myself?" The irony of it was not lost on me. There is no Kentucky law that guarantees survivors of domestic violence a lawyer to represent them in a divorce. By and large, if the survivor cannot pay for private representation, she (the survivors I work with are most often women) must navigate the court system on her own. I am always embarrassed to have to explain this to clients, even though I'm just the messenger.

Jeanette's astonishment only grew when I explained to her that not only did Mike get an attorney, but she would have to pay for it. Kentucky law requires the state to cover the cost of civil law attorneys only in rare circumstances, and in Jeanette's situation there was no provision for the courts to cover or waive this requirement. Whatever the bill for Mike's private lawyer turned out to be, Jeanette would be on the hook for it.

At first, I think, Jeanette didn't believe it could be true that she would actually have to pay for Mike's attorney. I look young for my age, and she probably thought I was confused about the law. Then the bill arrived, and she moved from denial to anger. Anger at the system that made her feel as though Mike was once again in control. Anger toward this law that seemed to value Mike's rights more than hers. Anger that, with everything going on in her life, she had to spend her time and money on Mike.

Jeanette was far from the only woman this law revictimized. I'd represented several women who had similar experiences. Often their husbands were in jail for violent crimes, drug charges, or crimes against a child. In order to divorce their husbands, these women had to come up with large sums of money to pay for guardians ad litem to represent their incarcerated spouses. This was true even though they could not afford private lawyers for themselves — the fact that I was representing them through Legal Aid was proof of that. I had heard tales from other parts of the state as well. One attorney who works in Owsley County knew a woman who couldn't get the judge to finalize her divorce until she paid thousands of dollars to cover her husband's guardian ad litem bill.

Eventually, Jeanette's divorce was finalized. She hugged me three times once the hearing was over. She and I had developed a good relationship; we weren't that far apart in age, and our conversations always flowed easily. I admired her tenacity. I was glad that she was moving on, but I was going to miss working with her.

The only matter remaining was to pay the guardian ad litem bill. I wanted Jeanette to have the freedom not to worry about it, so I found a litigation fund that was willing to help her cover the debt. These funds are limited, and not every woman in need can utilize them. But I don't know that Jeanette could have paid that bill without the assistance.

I had thought I would be able to move on from Jeanette's case — there were always new clients, and I was always hearing about horrific situations. But something about Jeanette's story stuck with me. It seemed so patently unfair — that our system of justice could perpetrate such *in*justice.

I met Jeanette at the same courthouse to sign the closing paperwork in her case. It had been several months since her divorce was finalized, and I was glad to hear all of the ways her life had improved. She had met a man who treated her and her son with kindness. She was working in a hospital. She seemed happy, relaxed. She smiled with her eyes.

I asked Jeanette if she would mind if I shared her story. "Names and details changed, of course," I told her. "I'll make sure nobody knows that it's you." She immediately said yes. She told me that if her story could make a difference for one woman, she was happy for me to share it in its entirety. Every client I've asked this question gives me the same answer: If my suffering can help someone else, I want to do what I can.

In 2018, I wrote an op-ed for a local paper. I told Jeanette's story — under a different name — and explained why the guardian ad litem system was so unfair in her case. We shouldn't live in a world where survivors of domestic violence have to pay for the attorneys of their incarcerated spouses. We shouldn't make women give money and advantages to the men who beat them.

I didn't expect much to happen after the article was published. I had written another op-ed a few months before, raging against the domestic relations commissioner fees and the ways they hurt poor people in rural Kentucky. A few of my attorney friends had mentioned the article over drinks, and commiserated with me about how unfair the system was, but that was it. I expected something similar from this article as well. I was losing faith that the system would ever change.

I was surprised when people began paying attention. The day the article was published, a local state legislator shared it on social media and announced that he would introduce legislation to remedy the situation. His name was Morgan McGarvey, and he called me the next day to brainstorm how we could make sure Jeanette's story didn't become a script that played out time and again in Kentucky courts. After we hung up, I called Jeanette to let her know about the development.

"You don't have to be involved," I told her, "and everyone will understand if you choose not to be." I didn't want Jeanette to feel pressure to come forward if she wasn't comfortable. She lived in a small town in rural Kentucky, and I understood why she might not want everyone knowing the details of her divorce.

"But I wanted to let you know that you are more than welcome to be a part of this process if you would like to," I continued. At the end of the day, the story I was telling belonged to Jeanette. There was no more powerful voice to tell it with than her own.

"I want to be a part of it," she declared.

Jeanette took it from there. People were interested in her story, and she was contacted by a variety of media outlets who wanted to learn more. Jeanette said yes to each and every request. She said yes to being interviewed by the local newspapers about her experience. She said yes to testifying before legislative committees. She said yes to going on television and showing the world pictures of her bruises from the night Mike had beaten her. Even when Mike's family and friends started putting pressure on her to keep quiet, she kept telling her story.

That legislative session was a particularly disheartening one in Kentucky. Republicans controlled the governorship, the state house, and the state senate. Very few Democratic bills were getting through, and Morgan McGarvey is a Democrat. At several points it seemed as though the bill might stall. I was worried that all of Jeanette's effort was going to be for naught.

But Jeanette's story was so powerful that there was no stopping the bill that now bore her name. People had seen her face, had come to associate it with the injustice she had endured. It passed both chambers of the state legislature, and the governor signed Jeanette's Law into being.

My experience with Jeanette was a powerful reminder about the importance of telling women's stories. Her voice led to tangible changes in the state law. Because of her bravery, other women's lives will be better.

It was also a reminder that things can get better. By the time I wrote that op-ed for the local newspaper, I was disheartened with the court system. I felt like I had failed so many clients: Peggy, Patsy, Roy, others. I had been raging into the abyss, screaming about injustice and unfairness and hearing nothing back but the echo of my own voice. It seemed like somebody, somewhere, had finally heard the shouts.

I had other small victories after Jeanette's Law. I was part of a team that appealed a rural judge who wouldn't waive the filing fee for expungement cases — the way to remove a criminal charge or conviction from a person's record. The filing fee for an expungement ranged between $100 and $500. Very few low-income Kentuckians are able to afford that, so, effectively, wealthier, often white, people convicted of crimes can get expungements, while poorer, often black, people cannot. This disparity and its racial connotation were particularly worrisome because Kentucky is one of two states that permanently ban felons from voting. As a result, Kentucky is number one in the nation for disproportionate disenfranchisement of people of color: 26 percent of African Americans in Kentucky cannot vote. The way the courts were applying the expungement law was only adding to this horrific disparity. When the reviewing circuit court agreed with us and ordered the district judge to waive the expungement filing fees for low-income Kentuckians, I danced around my tiny office.

These wins are small. There is a lot more work to be done in rural courts in Kentucky and, I imagine, in rural courts throughout Appalachia. There is never enough time, energy, or money to help everyone in need. I once met a woman who was married to a man she hadn't seen in seventeen years because she couldn't figure out how to get a divorce and couldn't afford an attorney to help her. Legal service agencies do the best they can. But the demand for services is great, and, when attorneys have to cover large geographic areas, it is impossible to help every person who qualifies.

But each small win is just that: a win. And each win is a reminder that things can change. These wins are also a reminder that people who have been victimized — be it by a spouse or by an unjust system — are nonetheless powerful. Some people portray survivors of domestic violence as weak; some people portray the women in Appalachia the same way. I think Jeanette's story illustrates the opposite. When given the right tools, support, and environment, these women are capable of changing the world.

CHAPTER 17

The Kentucky Democratic Party headquarters is an interesting bit of architecture. It's supposed to look like the state of Kentucky when you drive past it on the interstate. To me, it has always looked like the 1970s, with some strange angles and jarring peaks.

But, on this particular day, the building looked intimidating. I had been to Democratic headquarters only a few times in my life. I had always been a Democrat — minus a brief stint in my midtwenties when I thought I might be a Libertarian — but a Democrat of the casual variety. The kind who pays attention to the presidential elections every four years and likes to debate taxes and social programs over dinner.

And yet, here I was to interview as vice chair of the state party.

I hadn't become politically activated overnight. For a while, I thought the work I was doing as a Legal Aid attorney was enough to make a difference. I was going to save the world one person at a time, one family at a time, by providing legal services to those who needed them. I was going to help the people in front of me in the ways that were available to me.

Then November 2016 happened. I went to bed early on the night of the presidential election. I had been excited to vote for a woman earlier that day — the type of genuine excitement I had never felt about an election before. I called my mom as I drove in to work and told her, "Today's the day I get to vote for a female president of the United States — isn't that cool?"

I was watching the returns at home that evening — I wasn't engaged enough to know where to find an election party — and talking to Bryan on the phone. It was just after our first trip together, and we were still in that foggy, new-relationship glow. I didn't really pay attention to the returns until after we got off the phone. When I first noticed that Donald Trump was pulling ahead, I figured it was just a fluke. One of those weird results you see based on whatever smattering of states is in at the time. I started to tense up, and I decided there was no point in stressing over things unnecessarily. I went to sleep and figured that everything would be okay in the morning. I fell asleep with the TV on.

I woke up the next morning to the sound of shocked newscasters reading surprising headlines. Donald Trump had been elected president. I was immediately worried. Many of my relatives depended on the Affordable Care Act for health insurance coverage. Donald Trump had campaigned on platforms that would harm people I cared about. I went on my morning run without the usual news playing through my headphones.

The Appalachian counties in Kentucky voted overwhelmingly for Donald Trump in the 2016 election. He won 84 percent of the vote in Owsley County. Hillary Clinton carried only two of Kentucky's 120 counties: the ones with the two largest cities in the state.

After November 2016, I realized in a whole new way that elections mattered. It wasn't enough to save the world one family at a time. Elections are the way you make society into whatever vision of it you have. Winning elections is how things get better. I started to get more involved in politics.

When, two years later, the position of vice chair for the state Democratic Party opened, I never dreamed that I was qualified for it. I wasn't a party insider. I didn't know the latest political gossip. I had barely any political relationships. Yes, I knocked on doors for candidates and showed up at local Democratic club meetings, but I didn't even think about throwing my hat into the ring for the role. The vice chair was voted on by representatives throughout the state of Kentucky. Even though it was unpaid, a volunteer job, it seemed like a big deal.

Then a woman from Emerge Kentucky, an organization that trains women to run for office, sent me a message. "Why not apply?" she said. "Of course you're qualified. You should give it a try." I decided it couldn't hurt, and I filled out the application.

When I became a member of Emerge, Kentucky ranked forty-second in the nation for the number of females holding elected office. Of the 138 seats in the Kentucky state legislature, women held only 26. In 2018, Kentucky was ranked the sixth most sexist state in America. I'm not sure if sexism results in fewer elected women in Kentucky or vice versa — I'm sure they're related.

It's not that women lose when they run for elected office. In fact, the opposite is true. In 2016, the year Donald Trump was elected and Democrats took a beating in elections across the nation, Emerge Kentucky alumnae won 61 percent of their races. In the 2018 midterms, Kentucky elected ten new Democratic women to the state house. When women run, women win.

The problem is that women, particularly those from rural areas, don't run often enough. If no one had asked me, I certainly wouldn't have — at least not as early as I did. Getting involved in politics seemed intimidating, like something I needed far more experience to do — like there was a specialized language I didn't yet know. I was at the interview for vice chair that day only because someone had asked me to be. Someone had told me that I was qualified, that my voice was legitimate, valuable, and welcome. I ended up being elected vice chair of the state party.

A lot of people changed the way they looked at me after they found out I was "one of those political people." Some admired me for engaging — it turned out that people I never expected had the same viewpoints I did. For others, my involvement made them distrust me — a lot of people assume the worst of anyone in politics. And a few friendships withered away in today's polarized environment —

several Republican friends became more guarded around me, and I wasn't sure how to get back to our days of careless political banter, even though I tried to. I began to see what people were talking about when they claimed that our nation was becoming more divided.

I didn't always feel welcome at political events. The fact that I was a young woman made some people look past me. I was referred to as "that little girl" more times than I can count. There was still a sense in some places that politics is a blood sport, one that is better played by men. No one said that to me directly, but I heard it each time someone looked at me and said, "It must be so stressful for you to do all of this traveling. Does your husband mind you being away so much?"

But it was empowering to claim space for myself — to show up and say that my ideas mattered. When I spoke to groups, I talked about my roots in Eastern Kentucky and how the values I learned there shaped me. After one speech in a rural part of the state, a man brought his seven-year-old daughter up to talk to me. "Can I go to Harvard too?" the young girl asked me.

I told her, "There is nothing that's impossible for you to do." I wanted her to believe that as much as I did at her age.

As I traveled more and more, I realized that I wasn't the only woman doing this type of political work. In the mountains, I found a host of women engaged in politics in surprising and interesting ways. They weren't doing this work for the power or the ego. For them, politics was a tool to better their communities.

There was Sister Mary, a Catholic nun who was active in her Democratic Woman's Club. She had decided that one of her life missions was to win more voters in her county over to the Democratic Party, because she believed that Democratic policies would provide opportunities for the struggling members of her community. In the evenings, she would go to her Trump-voting neighbors' houses and invite herself to sit on the porch and chat a spell. When she asked her neighbors why they weren't Democrats, they often responded with something about abortion. Sister Mary made it clear then and there that "there is a difference between being pro-life and pro-birth. You can't call yourself pro-life if you want to cut children's health insurance and make it harder for working families to get by." She chuckled as she told me this, adding that she had great success in winning folks back to the Democratic tent. I'm guessing some of them just wanted this stubborn, fiery woman to get off of their porches.

Another woman, Victoria, was new to the mountains. She had moved there from a more urban area because she loved the beauty and the intimacy of a small town — she wanted to raise her family there. She believed that Democratic values were the best way for her community, in Estill County, to progress, but she had been told, "There are no Democrats in Estill County." She felt lonely and isolated after the 2016 election. She assumed that everyone around her was a Trump voter. Never one to accept information without questioning it, Victoria went and looked up the voter registration totals in her county. When she realized there were more than 4,000 registered Democrats nearby, she placed an ad in the local newspaper asking Democrats to come and join her new club.

At first, people were hesitant. Business leaders worried that people wouldn't come to their businesses; parents worried that other parents wouldn't let their kids play with their children. I've heard that some rural churches tell their members that if they vote Democrat, they're going to hell.

In small towns that lean heavily Republican, people worry they will face tangible repercussions for their Democratic affiliation.

Victoria grew the membership of her club astronomically. I went to one event where she had 250 people at a cookout on a Friday night. She had created a community. But this community was not isolated unto itself; Victoria formed meaningful and productive relationships with Republicans in the area. She told me, "In small towns you have to get along with your neighbors. Doesn't matter if they're a Democrat or a Republican, you still have to get your kids off the same school bus." On the last election night, members of both parties watched the results together.

I met Latoya, a young black woman running for office in a rural district in Western Kentucky, through Emerge. She was tall and stylish. She looked like she belonged on a runway in New York rather than in a small town in Kentucky. She grew up poor and black in a town that was mostly middle-class and white.

One day, at an event, Latoya came up to me and asked for advice. She was thinking about quitting her campaign. She was showing up at events in her area and felt like people weren't interested in meeting her —

like they didn't want to give her a chance to tell them who she was. She told me about one evening when a group of white men physically turned their backs on her to block her out of their conversations. She was afraid to knock on doors in some of the rural areas of her district without a white friend with her. "I'm not going to be a news story," she told me, "at least not *that* type of news story." She was exhausted from trying so hard and getting so little benefit in return.

As soon as she explained her frustrations to me, though, she was over it. In pretty much the next breath she told me, and herself, why she would keep doing the work she was doing. "I never had any role models that looked like me growing up. I didn't even have a black teacher. I'm doing this so some girl out there doesn't have to say the same thing one day."

There is intolerance — racism, sexism, homophobia — in the mountains. I once confronted Ruth's husband, Sonny, when he used a racial slur at a family dinner. He wasn't the only one. These things make me ashamed, of both my family and the communities that let them grow up with these beliefs. I know these actions are rooted in ignorance, but I also know ignorance is no excuse.

And I also remind myself that there are tolerant, accepting people in the mountains. I'm lucky to have known more people in rural Kentucky who are welcoming than who are not, although I recognize that for some the opposite is true. In 2018, the Democratic Woman's Club of Kentucky elected my friend Joanne, a transgender woman from rural Kentucky, first vice president — the holder of this title usually goes on to become president of the club the next year. And Aunt Ruth recently told me about two married women who moved into a holler nearby. When I asked her what she thought about that, she replied, "Well, Lord, honey — they ain't a-hurtin' nobody," and looked at me as if my question was one of the stupidest things she'd heard that month.

On one visit to Owsley County, Aunt Ruth and I went for a morning walk in the cemetery. "Do you think it's okay to walk here?" I asked her. I had once mistakenly cut through a cemetery in Louisville during one of my runs and been almost immediately chased out by a caretaker.

"Why, Lord yes," Aunt Ruth responded. "I bet they appreciate the company." As we walked along the path she pointed out a mound of dirt in the back corner. "That right there's an old slave cemetery. I started mowin' it a couple years ago. It didn't used to have no tombstones on it. But some of the women in town found a way to get money to put tombstones on it. I think it looks right pretty now."

It's certainly not enough — not any of it. Eastern Kentucky — and America — has a long way to go to be as tolerant as it should. But there are good people with good values in the mountains. And I think that's a start.

Not too long after Donald Trump's election, I asked Aunt Ruth why so many people in Owsley County liked him. I had gotten that question a lot, and it seemed like she was better suited to answer it than I was.

"People are flat-out crazy for Trump," she told me.

Sonny chimed in too. "People are plumb crazy for him. I ain't never seen anything like it."

"I think it's that people like that he talks like them," Aunt Ruth continued. "The way he talks makes it seem like he's for workin' folks."

Eastern Kentuckians used to think that the Democratic Party — the party that supported labor unions and social policies —

stood for working people. That's why Democratic registration still outnumbers Republican registration in many Eastern Kentucky counties. In Breathitt County, which shares a border with Owsley, 88 percent of registered voters are Democrats.

But these counties have voted increasingly in favor of Republicans over time. In 2016, 70 percent of voters in Breathitt County voted Republican. Maybe that's because voters thought the Democratic Party didn't deliver on its promises to make working people's lives better. Maybe it's because, in past years, the Democratic Party knew that it could win more votes in urban areas and didn't bother spending as much time in the mountains.

The new Democratic Party chair and I tried to do things differently. We believed in showing up and competing everywhere in the state, not just in the urban areas that are reliably blue. But Eastern Kentuckians are a proud people, and many hadn't forgotten the times they felt the Democratic Party hadn't shown up in the past.

And it goes without saying that some people are angry. Many people in Owsley County sit in front of their televisions night after night watching images of a world that feels foreign to them. They watch shows about the ultra-rich and ultra-famous, knowing that their lives will never look like those they see on their screens. People of both political parties have made a lot of promises to them over the years, yet other parts of America seem farther away from the mountains than ever before. They're not sure who to blame for the ways their lives aren't what they wish they were. It's easy to see why they were attracted to a political candidate like Donald Trump, who wanted to burn everything down.

But don't mistake this anger for unsophistication. On my last trip to Owsley County, Sonny spent ten minutes explaining to me why Donald Trump's trade policies had lowered the price you could get selling a load of junk in a nearby town. By the time he finished explaining steel and aluminum tariffs, my head was spinning.

I spent the most recent primary election day in Owsley County with Aunt Ruth. I had been in a nearby county for a meeting with Eula Hall — founder of the Mud Creek Clinic — who was hesitant to get together with me that Tuesday. "But it's Election Day," she said as though I should understand that all other work should come to a stop. Finally, she agreed to meet with me after I reassured her that I would show up late enough to give her plenty of time to cast her ballot in the morning.

Election Day, even in primary elections, is a big deal in Owsley County. After I'd finished meeting with Eula, Aunt Ruth and I went to the one sit-down restaurant in Booneville. The restaurant was packed with people interested in discussing politics, including the town's ninety-something-year-old mayor, who has been in office since 1959. I spoke with the mayor for a few minutes, and he told me all about the new grant for sidewalks that the city had won. We were interrupted by people throughout our brief conversation. One person wanted to congratulate him on the grant, another wanted to complain about something, still another wanted his thoughts on the elections. When I asked Aunt Ruth if the mayor was a Democrat or a Republican, she wasn't sure. Nobody nearby knew either.

People at the restaurant were aflutter with predictions about the election results: Who would win the local offices? How would the other side react if they lost? Would anybody get into a fistfight? About five minutes after the polls closed, Sonny started calling the clerk's office to get the results. "Well, do you know who won the magistrate race?" Sonny hollered. "Well, I guess I'll call you

351

back in a few more minutes, then. Let me know if y'all have the results." Aunt Ruth explained to me that people were no longer able to go to the courthouse to wait for the election returns because too many brawls had broken out over the years.

The voter turnout numbers in Owsley County reflect the passion that people feel for politics. Whereas only a little over 17 percent of voters in Jefferson County, where Louisville is located, turned out to vote on primary day, almost 47 percent of Owsley Countians showed up. And people aren't just engaged on Election Day. Aunt Ruth watched the Kavanaugh Supreme Court confirmation hearings in their entirety. When Sonny fell asleep, she shook him and said, "Wake up. We have to decide if that man is guilty or not." Afterward, she told me, "He's guiltier than sin."

Recently, I revisited the conversation about Donald Trump with Ruth and Mabel. We were at a family gathering, and we decided to talk politics while the men were outside grilling burgers. "Why do people in Owsley County like him so much?" I asked once again.

"Honey, I don't think they do anymore," Aunt Ruth told me. "People don't think he's done nothin' for no one. 'Specially not for the workin' people." She tilted her head. "I think people in Breathitt County still like him. But folks 'round here don't.

"And let me tell you somethin'," she continued, "he's gone and made women mad something awful. You can't make women mad like that — they'll show up at the polls is what they'll do!"

The numbers from the 2018 midterm elections support Aunt Ruth's claims that rural Kentuckians are increasingly less enamored with Donald Trump. Although Republicans still hold a super majority in the Kentucky state house and senate after the midterms, the Republican margin of victory shrank significantly. Democrats fell 23,000 votes short of taking back the state house in 2016. Just two years later, in 2018, they cut that vote deficit by 60 percent and fell only 9,000 votes short. We made these gains despite Donald Trump coming to Kentucky to campaign for Republican candidates.

And the Democrats flipped three state house seats in Eastern Kentucky, including the one that encompasses Owsley County. "Of course the Democrat won," Aunt Ruth told me. "That Republican wanted to merge our county with Lee County — we'd have lost 'bout a hundred jobs!" After the 2018 midterms, Eastern Kentucky was looking like one of the bluest parts of the state. Then again, polls still show that Donald Trump is popular in Kentucky, and I'm not sure how much the discontentment I hear people express will translate at the 2020 polls.

Mabel, who had been waiting eagerly for a break in the conversation, chimed in with her thoughts about Donald Trump. "I voted for him 'cause I didn't trust Hillary. But I don't have nothin' good to say about him anymore. The only thing he's done is make it so we don't have to pay the penalty for not havin' health insurance." She paused and thought. "It's not right, you know, makin' people buy health insurance. We couldn't afford it. They might as well have given everyone free health insurance. I wouldn't have minded that."

On paper, Owsley County looks like one of the most Republican counties in the state, maybe even in the nation. On the ground, though, the dialogue is different, more nuanced. My uncle Sonny is a Republican. "That's just how things are," he tells me. But he loves to talk politics with me, and has never disrespected my point of view. "Huh. I never thought about things thataway," he will say, his brow furrowed as he ponders. He agreed with Aunt Ruth's assessment of Brett Kavanaugh. He told me that he's worried about Donald Trump's impact on our nation. "Now, I'm not goin' to say it in public, you see, 'cause in some parts 'round here they might shoot you, but the way he's a-doin' things, it's just not right." He was genuinely distraught about the Trump administration's policy of separating migrant children from their families at the Mexico border.

Sonny puts signs in his yard for Democratic candidates who he believes in. He had a sign for the Democratic candidate for sheriff the last time I was there. These aren't national-level candidates, people he doesn't have a connection to. They are local people he knows and trusts. He believes that they will do right by him and his community.

For some reason, Sonny's yard signs make me feel hopeful. Maybe our politics aren't as divided as we think. Maybe we as a people aren't as divided as we think. And, maybe, we can still agree that our communities are more important than our politics.

CHAPTER 18

It rained on the day I married Bryan. Not a light, drizzly rain — that would've been kind of romantic. It downpoured — the kind of rain that hits you with its weight and soaks you through in seconds. I sat in my hotel room that morning watching the water fall down from the sky.

My mother was beside me on the couch, frantically checking her phone while trying to hide that franticness from me. She was in charge of my wedding; she had planned it down to the last detail. Bryan and I had both been busy at work, and neither of us had had the time to invest in wedding details. Plus, I don't think we cared about the specifics all that much. We were just happy to be getting married. My mother had been retired for several months, and she was looking for a project to take on. She was detail oriented, a hopeless romantic, and a big fan of Bryan. It made sense for her to take charge of the day.

She and my father insisted on paying for the wedding. They were proud of me, and they had the money to spare. My father had recently been promoted to associate dean at the University of Kentucky. His investment in education was continuing to pay off. I protested heavily — "The reasoning behind the bride's family paying is so problematic!" I exclaimed — but my mother and father wanted to give me the gift of a beautiful wedding. I tried to accept that gift gracefully.

My mother spent almost a year planning it. She provided us with an agenda of the day and what time things would happen. The décor was similarly well-thought-out. She had wanted mercury-glass instead of plain-glass votives because it would add more ambience to the room. I had argued with her, saying that any added ambience wouldn't be worth the extra money. She insisted, and she was right: The mercury glass did add a warm glow.

She was also right about the flowers. I had wanted to save money and do them myself by having wholesale flowers shipped in the evening before. She had put her foot down and told me she loved flowers and that she intended to get them from a professional florist. "I will not be staying up to midnight the day before my only daughter's wedding rehydrating flowers," she said with a look that told me I should stop arguing with her.

I thought about the women in my family a lot in the months leading up to the wedding. I thought about Granny and how it must've felt to marry a man she had known for only a few months. I had known Bryan for a year and a half, and still some people questioned why we were rushing into things. I knew almost everything about Bryan: what makes him laugh, what makes him sad, how to cheer him up after a stressful day at work. How different would it be to have discovered those things about him after having already committed to spending my life with him?

I also thought a lot about my mother — how she planned her wedding in just a few months and with a shoestring budget. She carried artificial flowers to save money. She knew my father, yes, but they were both still children on their wedding day. Bryan and I were in our thirties when we got married. We both had careers and graduate degrees. I imagine it would've felt different to have little idea of the people we would grow up to be.

It's an interesting image to think about,

the three of us lined up beside one another on our wedding days. Granny in her blue dress and house shoes, my mother in an off-the-rack white dress, me in a tailored gown, each of us standing next to the husband we chose. Granny next to a man she had known for just a few months, my mother next to a man she had agreed to marry three months before, me next to someone I had been engaged to for almost a year. Granny at fifteen, my mother at nineteen, me at thirty-one.

I wonder if looking at each of us on our wedding days can tell you something about the way we progressed as a family — the way each of us built on what was given to us by the generation before. We gained something because of their hard work. But I wonder if we lost something as well: identity, community, connection to a place and to one another.

I pulled myself from my thoughts as my bridesmaids began to arrive in the hotel suite to get ready for the day. While we had our hair styled, my mother slipped into her dress. It was the first long dress she had ever worn. She'd ordered a dozen online before deciding on this one. It was a deep plum that complemented her blue, still-sparkling eyes. She looked young, beautiful, and at home in it. My friends who met her at the rehearsal dinner the night before couldn't believe that she was old enough to have a daughter in her thirties. I reminded them that by the time my mother was my age, she had a preteen daughter.

I don't remember much about walking down the aisle. That part was a blur. But I do remember seeing my mother standing at the end. She mouthed the words "I love you" as I walked past her and stopped next to Bryan.

Aunt Ruth was not at the wedding. None of my relatives from Owsley County were there. We invited them, but we knew they wouldn't come. "Louisville may as well be Beijing as far as they're concerned," I explained to Bryan when he asked me why they weren't on the list of confirmed guests. They don't have cellphones; I don't know that they have ever seen a parking garage. They don't know how to get around in a city the size of Louisville, let alone how to use a GPS to guide them. We assured them that it was okay, that we would find time to celebrate with them later.

I missed them that day. The guests reflected nearly all of the important places in my life. I had friends from Yale, London, and Harvard; my new friends in Louisville were there as well. But Owsley County wasn't represented, and I couldn't shake the feeling that an important piece of who I am was missing.

I celebrated my marriage with my Owsley County family a few months later, on a beautiful Saturday in July. The sun was bright but not oppressive, and the humidity was lower than normal. My mother had reserved the one event space in Booneville, a renovated barn filled with folding furniture and burlap tablecloths. She had glued lace onto a few vases and filled them with Costco flowers. The barn looked beautiful.

I wore my same wedding dress. I didn't want to spend the money to buy a second one, but I also wanted my Owsley County family to experience as close to the original wedding as possible. Not so much for their sake as for mine. There had been a hole in my wedding day that I needed them to fill.

I had a moment of panic when I first got to the barn and opened the dress bag. The dress had a corset, which had originally been laced with a delicate satin ribbon. That ribbon had gotten lost somewhere between Louisville and Owsley County, and I had nothing to hold my dress together. "Do we have fishing twine? A shoelace? Anything?"

I asked my mother. I knew that the rest of the family would be arriving soon.

She tapped a finger to her chin and thought. "I've got something even better," she said as she disappeared down the stairs. She came back with a roll of jute twine, a thick brown rope used for gardening and other odd jobs. At first the twine was too wide to fit through the corset holes, but my mother stripped and separated it until it slipped through easily. "See? I told you we'd figure it out," she said once the dress was fully tied. I put a lace jacket over the top part of the dress before going downstairs. I wasn't sure my uncles were ready to see me in a strapless dress.

My family members began to arrive around noon, each one with a dish of food. I love that special occasions in Eastern Kentucky are marked by a potluck — it's a more active and communal way to celebrate. Aunt Ruth brought corn bread, soup beans, and my favorite banana pudding. Mabel brought chicken and dumplings, shuck beans, and potato salad. I lost track of who brought the rest of the food. The table was overflowing.

The barn soon filled with noise and energy. Uncle Dale sang bluegrass tunes, and I tried to clog in my wedding dress. My dad manned the grill out back, filling aluminum tins with burgers and hotdogs. At some point Aunt Ruth hollered for people to start eating. In between shouts she turned to me. "You sure make a pretty bride" — she gave me a meaningful look — "but you go put on some comfy blue jeans whenever you're ready. It's hot in here." My mother, eyes full of happy tears, introduced me to Verlene, her friend from high school, whom she hadn't seen in over thirty years. Verlene had heard that Wilma's daughter was having a wedding reception in town — news still travels fast in Booneville — and decided to stop by. My relatives had put out the word that anyone and everyone was welcome at the wedding barn that day.

Bryan's family was at the wedding that day too. His mother, brother, and one of his aunts had driven from Louisville because they wanted to get to know my extended family. I took them from table to table, introducing them. When I got to Uncle Dale I teased, "This is the uncle you'd want to know if you ever needed to get rid of a body."

"I got rid of my body years ago!" Dale shot back, patting his rounded stomach. "I think it's in the witness protection program — to protect the witnesses!" Bryan's family laughed. Everyone relaxed.

Billy, my cousin Melissa's son, spent most of the day in the green space behind the barn, back where my dad was grilling. Billy's gotten quieter over the years, and he seemed uncomfortable in the wedding barn that day. He looks to everyone else for cues and acceptance. When he does speak, his voice is soft and most of his sentences sound like a question. Recently my mother asked him if he'd given any more thought to what he'd like to study after high school. When she asked him what he enjoyed learning, he looked surprised, as if no one had ever asked him that question before. "I suppose I like building things," he said after a pause. She told him that there were ways to go to school and make a career out of that, and he sat silent for several minutes. "Maybe I'll just do that," he said softly.

Melissa wasn't there that day. I had invited her, but I knew she wouldn't come. I've been trying to reconnect with her, extending invitations through my mom to go to lunch with us or meet up when I'm in Owsley County. I heard she has traced our family's mountain roots back to the 1700s, and I want to talk to her about what she's learned. But I've never heard from her and I don't really know how else to reach out.

One relative told me that Melissa wants nothing to do with me because she's jealous: "She can't figure out why her life didn't turn out like yours. She thinks she deserved it." I want to tell Melissa that I wrestle with the same question.

Before the reception ended, I asked Aunt Ruth if she would take a picture with me. I wanted to have it to remember the day. At first she hemmed and hawed. "Honey, I ain't dressed up," she told me. She was wearing blue jeans and an American flag T-shirt.

"I'm the only one dressed up here," I responded truthfully. "And I want a picture with my Aunt Ruth."

"Well, okay then," she said matter-of-factly. I handed Sonny my cellphone and showed him how to use it. After I explained to him several times that the Home key was not what you pushed to take a picture, he finally managed to capture an image that wasn't terribly crooked. In that picture, Aunt Ruth looks mostly proud, and a little bit happy.

Later that evening, Bryan and I drove to a nearby state park, where we were staying the night in a cabin. I had heard that there was a hoedown that night, and I wanted Bryan to have the full Eastern Kentucky wedding experience. He gave me a suspicious look when I first told him about it, but he finally agreed: "If square dancing will make you happy, I'll give it a try."

My parents, his mother, and his aunt joined us. My dad and Bryan drove to a barbecue joint a few miles away to get us all sandwiches. Earlier that day my mother had hidden a couple of bottles of wine in a cooler in the back of her car. Now, miles away from her family's prying eyes, we sat on a porch and drank it as the sun set over the mountains. My mother had recently told Ruth that a doctor said drinking wine might help her medical condition. "Well," Ruth said thoughtfully, "it might, just might, be good for you."

"Your relatives are so fun," Bryan's mother said to me that evening. "Now, I couldn't always understand what they were saying. But they are such nice people." Bryan shot me an I-told-you-so look from across the porch. The party had gone well.

Soon the sound of fiddle playing wafted up the hill from the valley. "I think the hoedown is starting!" I said excitedly. "We best get moving if we're going to make it." Bryan squeezed my hand as we walked down the hill toward the music. We all danced until well after dark. We didn't know the steps to many of the dances, but that wasn't important. My dad and Bryan's mom joined in the square dancing. My mother sat on the sidelines with my dog while the rest of us do-si-do'd and did something resembling clogging.

The next morning, Bryan and I hiked to the top of a nearby mountain. The bright green hills rolled off into the distance as far as we could see. "I like being in the mountains," Bryan said. "We should come here more often." I nodded.

The mountains haven't changed much over time. They are the same today as they have been for generations. I'm less sure if my family has changed. On the outside, it looks like we have. Like each generation has seen more, shifted more, than the one before. Maybe it even looks like we have each become less connected to the mountains. But, when we're together, it doesn't feel like we're that far apart. I still feel like I am the same as my mother, as my aunt Ruth, as my Granny. I feel connected to the same hills and values that they did.

I want to come to the mountains more. On the day of our wedding reception, I asked Aunt Ruth to keep an eye out for small farms for sale in Owsley County. I'd like to have a formal way to belong there again, even though I know that I will never truly belong in the same way. I have grown, and I have changed, but I will always remember the hills that I came from.

EPILOGUE

"I love you, honey," Aunt Ruth says, hugging me close. "Your mama loves you too." I look at the cherrywood casket, draped with the brightest flowers my father and I could find, and my eyes fill with tears.

The day after I finished this book, my mother died. Bryan and I had bought a house a couple of weeks before, and my mother was driving from Berea to Louisville to help us with home-related tasks. She had made that drive several times that week, helping us to pack, unpack, and get our new place in order. That day, she was rear-ended by a semitruck on the interstate. It has been almost a week since she passed, and it still doesn't seem real. I can't imagine how life can keep on moving without her.

My mother believed in joy, and she always said that she wanted a party to celebrate her life when she died — she didn't want us sitting around being sad. So that's what we are trying to do today, throw a party in her honor. We found a blue-grass band to play mountain hymns during her church service, and we invited everyone to join us for food afterward. There is far too much of it, and I know that my mother would be pleased by that fact. Tomorrow we will bury her on a hill near Berea College, looking out on the rising Appalachians. I miss her already.

Aunt Ruth arrived at the church in a simple black knee-length dress, the fanciest outfit I've ever seen her in. Now, during the service, she sits behind me, patting my shoulder throughout. Just before I go up to give the eulogy, she plucks a piece of fuzz off my shoulder and smooths the back of my dress. She nods at me in a matter-of-fact way as if to say "Well, get along with it." But I can see tears in her eyes. I avoid her gaze so as not to break down crying.

My father was the one to call Ruth and tell her that my mom had died. Ruth must have been devastated, because all my father will say about that phone call is that it was "the roughest one." But around me, Ruth puts on a stoic face. I think she is trying to be strong for me, for my mother. There is a deep sadness in her eyes, though, and her voice, usually all lilt and melody, now sounds flat.

Melissa is at the service too. She sent me a message the day after my mother died and said we needed to stay in better touch, that the family was shrinking, and that it was up to us to keep it going. She told me once again how much she enjoyed coming to Berea when she was young, and we talked about getting together sometime soon. I hope we follow through. She has been kind this past week, checking on me and my father and asking what she can do to help.

There is a whole Owsley County contingent at the church today, not just family, but my mother's friends and acquaintances, some she hadn't seen in decades. At the celebration, they tell me stories about her as a young woman and give me hugs that last just a little too long. Several families from the Child Development Lab are there as well, and they tell me how much my mother changed their lives. "She taught me to be a better parent," one woman says.

I tell Bryan that I wish my mother had the chance to teach me that exact thing as we're driving back to my parents' home after the service. I am almost nineteen weeks pregnant, and one of my first thoughts when I learned my mother died was to question how I would raise this child without her. She was going to come and stay with us after I had the baby and watch her grandchild during the day once I went back to work. I felt comforted knowing that I would have her close by as I tackled this next life phase. I bragged about her like she was my secret weapon: "I know it's hard to do it all," I told my friends, "but I have my mom to help me." I feel like my foundation has suddenly and unexpectedly disintegrated to dust.

Bryan pulls me close and kisses the top of my head. "She already taught you to be a parent," he says. "She raised you. She's in you. She gave you everything you need to know."

Later in the evening, I am sitting in my childhood bedroom looking at pictures. It's the same stack of photographs my father and I went through a few days before, picking our favorites to blow up into poster-sized prints to set around the church. My mother would have wanted people to remember her as she was in those images: smiling, happy, with her family. That is how I want to remember her, and that is why I'm thumbing through these photos once again. Seeing her wide smile and sparkling eyes gives me comfort. It makes it feel as though she's not so far away.

Each memory is there in that stack: her

holding me as a newborn, reading to me as a child, waving at the camera as she stands in front of the South African ocean. I'm struck once again by how young she looks throughout it all. I'm also struck by the bends and pivots in her life path, the evolution and expansion of her world.

I take the picture of her in her high school graduation robes and place it next to one of her on my wedding day. You can see it in her graduation photo, the hope and nervousness she felt leaving the mountains. Her smile is subdued and her eyes are wide. I'm glad that she looks so happy on my wedding day, nearing the end of the journey she set out on all of those years ago. Her smile is radiant.

This wasn't the type of tribute to my mother I wanted this book to be. I wanted it to be something that she and I shared together, continued to share together. We were going to celebrate when it came out. She said she would buy the nicest bottle of champagne she could find.

I suppose in some ways we did get to share this book. Over the course of my writing it, my mother and I had countless conversations about her life, her memories, and our family. She gave me her story to tell, entrusted me to share it with the world. A couple of months ago she read a draft of it, and she told me that she felt honored. She called herself a "proud hill woman." I hope that the other women I've written about here feel the same.

We talked a lot about what it means to be a hill woman during these past few months. We told each other stories about the fire, grace, and grit that we saw in the mountains. We talked a lot about Ruth, about their relationship. "I called Ruth today," my mother told me one Sunday evening after she'd read the draft. "I never thanked her for all she'd done for me growing up." She paused, her voice heavy with emotion. "I told her I appreciated it. I told her she changed my life."

My mother and I agreed that more needed to be done for the mountains, for the struggling families there. We tried to figure out what that looked like. I told her that when I started writing this book, I thought I was doing it to find answers to questions like, What is the future of the Appalachian economy? and What should we do to move the region forward? I wanted to understand the past and the present and use that understanding to influence the future. I hoped that the writing process would be a funnel; that by pouring in all of my experiences I would be left with more narrow, streamlined thoughts coming out the other side.

But this book is now complete, and I don't have all the answers I'd hoped to. I still struggle with how to balance many delicate and competing concerns: talking about the problems Appalachia faces while highlighting its strengths; recognizing the importance of tradition while still supporting innovative change; encouraging community-driven solutions along with bringing outside resources to the region. I wish I had some more solid conclusions to share, but, in the end, it's the complexities of Appalachia and the people who live here that need sharing the most.

Today more than ever, I'm glad I've told these stories. I hope they have shown people the surprising nuances of the region and its problems, so often reduced to a singular stereotype. I hope they have made voices from the mountains ring louder and helped people see the potential that exists here. I hope they bring attention to an area that we often allow ourselves to overlook. The people here deserve that.

But, most important, I'm glad I've told these stories because there's now a piece of my mother that lives in these pages. She would want the world to understand her as a hill woman, to see the hope and joy in her journey and life. She would want people to take something of value from her story, from our family's story. It's a tale of struggle, change, and success that could be told more often if we, as a people, a country, a community, put in the effort to make it happen.

I know I haven't told every story here perfectly. This book is born from memory, both mine and others'. Memory is a fickle and faulty tool, and I'm sure that there are inaccuracies in these pages. In some places, I've purposefully changed details, altering names and minor facts to protect the identities of people who wish to avoid the spotlight. Sometimes I've changed the order of events to help the narrative run more smoothly. But I've done my best not to change the character of any story. It's important to me that I get things as right as possible.

As I reach for another pile of photographs, I feel a slight tap against my stomach, a tiny push that causes me to instinctively place my hand on my lower abdomen. I felt my baby boy kick for the first time the day after my mother died. I like to think that at some point the two of them chatted for a few minutes as they passed each other, somewhere on the path between heaven and earth. I know that the two of them had a connection. When I told my mother I was pregnant, she responded, "I know. You'll think I'm crazy, but I was praying a few months ago, and I just knew that my grandchild's soul was on its way here." The morning she died she told me that she wanted him to call her Nana.

Here's what I will someday tell my son about his nana Wilma: I will tell him that she was kind, warm, and more loving than anyone I ever knew; that she did things that made her scared and created opportunities for her daughter; that she loved her family fiercely and gave people more grace than they deserved. I will make sure he knows that she loved him.

I'll tell him about the other hill women who helped form him too. I'll tell him about Granny and Ruth, about how they valued education and sacrificed so that my mother could have it. I'll explain how their love and hard work led to the life we have now. I'll make sure he knows never to underestimate a mountain woman.

Part of me is scared that my mother was the thread that tied us to the mountains, and that without her my son and I will drift farther from the hills. I don't want that to happen. There is so much to gain here. I'll tell him about our family's roots and try to make him feel anchored in the mountains. I want him to be grounded in the hills, but also free to move beyond them.

I flip over the next photograph in the stack and pause to take it in. It is a picture of the old house on Cow Creek. The roof is still green, and the yard is alive with red and orange bushes. It's fall, and the front field is full of harvest remnants. The mountains rise up in the distance. I close my eyes and I am there once again. The sense of home and family washes over me. I feel my mother's presence nearby.

"I get it, Mom," I whisper to myself. "I'll keep going back." I'll remember the places and the stories. I'll honor her and the others like her. I won't forget the hills or the women who made them home.

ACKNOWLEDGMENTS

This book would not have been possible without the help of my mother, Wilma, who spent countless hours talking with me about her life and her memories. We were partners in this project. I'm thankful I can share her story.

To Ruth, Sonny, and the many other family members who helped with this book: Thank you. I have a better sense of who I am and where I came from because of our conversations. To my cousin "Melissa": I'm so glad that we have reconnected in these past months. Thank you for being so supportive and kind as I have navigated becoming a mother.

I am so thankful to have had an amazing team of women to guide me throughout this process. To Emily at Ballantine: You have been the best editor that I could've hoped for. Thank you for believing in this project from the beginning and shaping this book into what it has become. Jamie at WME: Thank you for being there beside me every step of the way. To the rest of the Ballantine team: Thank you for all you've done.

I owe a special thank-you to my husband, Bryan. You enthusiastically embraced this adventure and never once complained about all of the weekends I spent holed up writing. To my father, Orlando: Thank you for your unwavering support.

To the wonderful women who read early versions of the book and weighed in (Josie, Abby, Bailey, Brooke, Gretchen, and Kelsey): Thank you for being incredibly kind as readers and as friends. Thank you to Theo for being my constant sounding board and to Mike for all of your thoughtful advice.

Finally, to all the hill women past, present, and future: Thank you for shaping and inspiring me. This book belongs to you.

SELECTED SOURCES

Erin Arcipowski, et al. "Clean Water, Clean Life: Promoting Healthier, Accessible Water in Rural Appalachia." online library .wiley.com/doi/pdf/10.1111/j.1936-704X .2017.3248.x. *Journal of Contemporary Water Research and Education.* August 2017.

Bill Atkins. "Kentucky's Coal Industry Is Replete with 'Boom or Bust' History." www.nkytribune.com/2015/01/bill-atkins -kentuckys-coal-industry-is-replete-with -boom-or-bust-history-war-on-coal-is-a -myth/. *Northern Kentucky Tribune.* January 13, 2015.

Natasha Bach. "Thousands of Kentucky Residents Won't Be Able to Vote on Tuesday. Here's Why." fortune.com/2018/11/ 05/kentucky-felon-voting-rights/. *Fortune.* November 5, 2018.

Berea College. "Fact Sheet." www.berea .edu/wp-content/uploads/2015/09/Berea

-by-the-Numbers-2016.pdf.

Bonnie Berkowitz and Tim Meko. "Appalachia Comes Up Small in Era of Giant Coal Mines." www.washingtonpost.com/graphics/national/coal-jobs-in-appalachia/?utm_term=.c71b150d2a37. *The Washington Post.* May 5, 2017.

Nathan Bomey. "Thousands of Farmers Stopped Growing Tobacco After Deregulation Payouts." www.usatoday.com/story/money/2015/09/02/thousands-farmers-stopped-growing-tobacco-after-deregulation-payouts/32115163/. *USA Today.* September 2, 2015.

Patricia Buchanan, Vicky K. Parker, Ruth Zajdel. "Birthin' Babies: The History of Midwifery in Appalachia." files.eric.ed.gov/fulltext/ED464795.pdf.

Kathryn Casteel. "There Is More Than One Opioid Crisis." fivethirtyeight.com/features/there-is-more-than-one-opioid-crisis/. FiveThirtyEight. January 17, 2018.

Gina Castlenovo. "Mary Breckinridge." www.truthaboutnursing.org/press/pioneers/breckinridge.html.

Elizabeth Catte. *What You Are Getting Wrong About Appalachia.* Cleveland: Belt Publishing, 2018.

Center on Trauma and Children. "Grandparents as Parents: Investigating the Health and Well-Being of Trauma-Exposed Families." www.uky.edu/CTAC/sites/www.uky.edu.CTAC/files/UK_CTAC_report.pdf. University of Kentucky. 2014.

Centers for Disease Control. "Drug Overdose Mortality by State." www.cdc.gov/nchs/pressroom/sosmap/drug_poisoning_mortality/drug_poisoning.htm. National Center for Health Statistics. Last accessed February 22, 2019.

Luke Ciancarelli. "Report Shows Income Inequality at Yale." yaledailynews.com/blog/2017/02/03/report-shows-income-inequality-at-yale/. *Yale Daily News.* February 3, 2017.

J. E. Cornwall, et al. "Risk Assessment and Health Effects of Pesticides Used in Tobacco Farming in Malaysia." academic.oup.com/heapol/article-abstract/10/4/431/730387?redirectedFrom=PDF. *Health Policy and Planning.* December 1, 1995.

Theresa DiDonato. "These Are the Best (and Worst) Ages to Get Married." www.psychologytoday.com/us/blog/meet-catch-and-keep/201606/these-are-the-best-and-worst-ages-get-married. *Psychology Today.* June 1, 2016.

Bill Estep. "Coal Jobs Have Dropped in

Eastern Kentucky. Income Has Followed, New Report Shows." www.kentucky.com/news/state/article216946520.html. *Lexington Herald-Leader.* August 18, 2018.

———. "Many Hoped for a Rebound in Kentucky Coal Jobs Under Trump. It Hasn't Happened." www.kentucky.com/news/state/article216363175.html. *Lexington Herald-Leader.* August 9, 2018.

———. " 'Nobody to Pick From': How Opioids Are Devastating the Workforce in Eastern Kentucky." www.kentucky.com/news/state/article213189309.html. *Lexington Herald-Leader.* June 27, 2018.

———. "Trump Promised to Put Coal Miners Back to Work. Kentucky Has Fewer Coal Jobs Now." www.kentucky.com/news/state/article221408290.html. *Lexington Herald-Leader.* November 9, 2018.

Gwynn Guilford. "The 100-year Capitalist Experiment That Keeps Appalachia Poor, Sick, and Stuck on Coal." qz.com/1167671/the-100-year-capitalist-experiment-that-keeps-appalachia-poor-sick-and-stuck-on-coal/. *Quartz.* December 30, 2017.

"Health Disparities in Appalachia." www.arc.gov/assets/research_reports/ Health_Disparities_in_Appalachia_August_2017

.pdf. The Cecil G. Sheps Center for Health Services Research and the Appalachian Regional Commission. August 2017.

Kentucky Educational Television. *Settlement Schools of Appalachia.* www.ket.org/education/resources/settlement-schools-appalachia/.

"Kentucky Health News." kyhealthnews.blogspot.com/2017/01/meth-was-more-prevalent-in-dry-counties.html. January 10, 2017.

G. Khairy, et al. "Bilateral Breast Cancer: Incidence, Diagnosis and Histological Patterns." *Saudi Medical Journal.* 26(4). April 2005.

Nadia Kounang. "The Kentucky County Where the Water Smells Like Diesel." cnn.com/2018/03/30/health/kentucky-water-crisis/index.html. CNN. March 30, 2018.

Nikita Lalwani. "Tracing the Elite Law Cycle." yaledailynews.com/blog/2011/04/18/up-close-tracing-the-elite-law-cycle/. *Yale Daily News.* April 18, 2011.

Kat Lonsdorf. "Kentucky County Water Crisis." www.npr.org/2018/09/13/647559499/kentucky-county-water-crisis. NPR. September 13, 2018.

Michael G. Meyer, et al. "Cultural Perspectives Concerning Adolescent Use of Tobacco and Alcohol in the Appalachian Mountain Region." www.ncbi.nlm.nih .gov/pmc/articles/PMC2409582/. *Journal of Rural Health.* June 4, 2008.

Jerry Mitchell and Laura Ungar. "Drugs Kill More Americans Than Guns and Cars. Kentucky Was Ground Zero from the Start." www.courier-journal.com/ story/news/investigations/2018/01/28/ kentucky-ground-zero-opioid-epidemic/ 1069608001/. *The Courier Journal.* January 28, 2018.

Lara Moody, Emily Satterwhite, and Warren Bickel. "Substance Use in Rural Central Appalachia: Current Status and Treatment Considerations." www.ncbi.nlm.nih.gov/ pmc/articles/PMC5648074/. *Rural Mental Health.* April 1, 2017.

Johnny Noble. "Inside America's Poorest County." www.seeker.com/inside-americas -poorest-county-photos-1766208288 .html. *Seeker.* December 12, 2012.

Emma Ockerman. "African Americans in Appalachia Fight to Be Seen as a Part of Coal Country." www.washingtonpost.com/ news/post-nation/wp/2017/08/10/african -americans-in-appalachia-fight-to-be-seen -as-a-part-of-coal-country/?noredirect= on&utm_term=.7529103643b7. *The Washington Post.* August 10, 2017.

Erica Peterson. "New Research Group Aims to Shed Light on Appalachian Health Disparities." wfpl.org/new-research-group -aims-to-shed-light-on-appalachian-health -disparities/. WFPL Radio. August 7, 2017.

Sarah Riley. "Kentucky Named One of the Most Sexist States — And It's Hurting Women." www.courierjournal.com/story/ news/local/2018/08/30/kentucky-named -among-most-sexist-states/1134616002/. *The Courier Journal.* August 30, 2018.

Cassady Rosenblum. "Hillbillies Who Code." www.theguardian.com/us-news/ 2017/apr/21/tech-industry-coding-ken tucky-hillbillies. *The Guardian.* April 21, 2017.

Shaunna Scott. "Grannies, Mothers and Babies: An Examination of Traditional Southern Appalachian Midwifery." anthrosource.onlinelibrary.wiley.com/doi/ pdf/10.1525/cia.1982.4.2.17.

Jason Sumich. "It's All Legal Until You Get Caught: Moonshining in the Southern Appalachians." anthro.appstate.edu/research/ field-schools/ethnographic-and-linguistic -field-schools/summer-2007-alleghany -county/its. Appalachian State University. Summer 2007.

This American Life. "Episode 550: Three

Miles." www.thisamericanlife.org/550/
transcript. NPR. March 13, 2015.

George Torok. *A Guide to Historic Coal Towns of the Big Sandy River Valley.* Knoxville: University of Tennessee Press, 2004.

United States Census Bureau. "Owsley County, Kentucky." www.census.gov/quickfacts/fact/table/owsleycountyken tucky/BZA115216. Last accessed October 1, 2018.

Alexia Walters. "Moonshine Operation Found in Tow Truck Company Building." lex18.com/news/covering-kentucky/2018/08/30/moonshine-operation-found-in-tow-truck-company-building/. Lex18 News. August 30, 2018.

Gillian B. White. "The Quiet Struggle of College Students with Kids." www.theatlantic.com/business/archive/2014/12/the-quiet-struggle-of-college-students-with-kids/383636/. *The Atlantic.* December 11, 2014.

Bob Woods. "This Kentucky Coal Town Is Fighting for Survival Long After the War on Coal Is Over." www.cnbc.com/2018/03/29/the-kentucky-coal-town-fighting-to-survive-after-coal-mining-closings.html. CNBC. March 31, 2018.

Will Wright, Caity Coyne, and Molly Born. "Stirring the Waters: Investigating Why

Many in Appalachia Lack Reliable, Clean Water." www.kentucky.com/news/local/watchdog/article222656895.html. *Lexington Herald-Leader.* December 26, 2018.

Lawrence Yun. "Why Homeownership Matters." www.forbes.com/sites/lawrenceyun/2016/08/12/why-homeownership-matters/#593ffe42480f. *Forbes.* August 12, 2016.

ABOUT THE AUTHOR

Cassie Chambers grew up in Eastern Kentucky. She graduated from Yale College, the Yale School of Public Health, the London School of Economics, and Harvard Law School, where she was president of the Harvard Legal Aid Bureau, a student-run law firm that represents low-income clients. After law school, Chambers received a Skadden Fellowship to return to Kentucky to work with domestic violence survivors in rural communities. She lives in Louisville with her husband, Bryan; their dog, Brixton; and their cat, Spaghetti.

cassiechambers.com
Twitter: @cassiehchambers

The employees of Thorndike Press hope you have enjoyed this Large Print book. All our Thorndike, Wheeler, and Kennebec Large Print titles are designed for easy reading, and all our books are made to last. Other Thorndike Press Large Print books are available at your library, through selected bookstores, or directly from us.

For information about titles, please call:
  (800) 223-1244

or visit our website at:
  gale.com/thorndike

To share your comments, please write:
  Publisher
  Thorndike Press
  10 Water St., Suite 310
  Waterville, ME 04901